MEL BAY PRESENTS

SONGS OF IRELAND

103 Favourite Irish and Irish-American Songs

A Note From Jerry Silverman

A tune is more lasting than the song of the birds.
A word is more lasting than the riches of the world.
                                    –Irish proverb

The songs of a people do more than just recount the story of the people. They *are* the people. Irish songs are so intertwined with the long, sad tale of Ireland that even the happy songs seem to be (in the words of another oppressed people) "laughin' just to keep from cryin.' "

Outlaws, lovers, farmer, drinkers, sailors, yarn spinners, soldiers, emigrants, revolutionaries . . . what a cast of characters! What a wealth of words and music and more words and more music!

They struggled for some 800 years against Britain — losing battle after battle, and finally winning the war. They left in the millions for "Americay" — only to find new battles to fight, finally winning that war, as well.

What we have here, in some small way, is a musical chronicle of those struggles and those voyages. From the polished lines of Moore and Yeats, to the rollicking rhymes of Percy French, to the anguished cry of the wife upon seeing her crippled husband back from the wars, from Bendemeer's Stream to Brooklyn City . . . and all the good times and hard times in between.

A recording of the music in this book is now available. The publisher strongly recommends the use of this recording along with the text to insure accuracy of interpretation and ease in learning.

Contents

This beautiful love song has crossed the waters between Ireland and Scotland more than once—and in both directions.

Will You Go, Lassie, Go?

Oh the sum-mer time is com-ing,___ And the trees are sweet - ly bloom-ing,___ And the wild moun-tain thyme___ grows a-round the bloom-ing heath-er, Will ye go,___ Las - sie go, And we'll all go to-geth-er,___ To pluck wild moun-tain thyme___ all a-round the bloom - ing heath-er, Will ye go,___ las - sie, go.

E   A   E
I will build my love a tower
      A   E
Near yon pure crystal fountain,
  A E   C♯m
And on it I will build
      F♯m   A
All the flowers of the mountain. *Chorus*

      E   A   E
If my true love she were gone,
      A   E
I would surely find another,
      A   E   C♯m
Where wild mountain thyme
      F♯m   A
Grows around the bloomin' heather. *Chorus*

3

Kilgary Mountain

Elizabethan thoughts on Ireland (1562): ". . . Idle men of loose demeanor [such as rhymers, bards and dice players must not be permitted to travel through Munster]. . . . And as those rhymers by their ditties and rhymes, made for divers lords and gentlemen in Ireland, in commendation and high praise of extortion, rebellion, rape, rapine and other injustice, encourage those lords rather to follow those vices than to abandon them [the lords and gentlemen must not pay for these verses. If they did they would be fined double the amount paid.]"

A map of Ireland will show no prominence called Kilgary Mountain. The English complained about the "misty geography" of Irish place names. We are, in this ballad, in the Cork and Kerry Mountains. Indeed, another version begins: "As I was going over the far-famed Kerry Mountains. . . ."

As I was a-walkin' up-on Kil-ga-ry Moun-tain, I met with Col'-nel Pep-per, and his mon-ey he was count-ing. I drew up me pis-tols and I rat-tled up me sa-ber, say-ing, "Stand and de-liv-er, for I am a bold de-ceiv-er," Mush-a-ring-um dur-um dah, Whack fol the dad-dy, oh, Whack fol the dad-dy, oh, There's whis-ky in the jar.

C / Am
The money in me hand, it looked so neat and jolly,
F / C Am
I took it right straight home, for to give to my Molly;
C / Am
She swore that she loved me and she never would deceive me,
F / C Am
But the devil's in the women and they always lie so easy. *Chorus*

C / Am
I went to me chambers to prepare myself for slumber,
F / C Am
To dream of gold and girls, and sure it is no wonder;
C / Am
But Molly took me pistols and she filled them up with water,
F / C Am
And she sent for Colonel Pepper to make ready for a slaughter. *Chorus*

C / Am
I woke next morning early, between six and seven,
F / C Am
With guards around me bed in both numbers odd and even;
C / Am
I flew to me pistols, but alas, I was mistaken,
F / C Am
I couldn't shoot the water and a pris'ner I was taken. *Chorus*

C / Am
They threw me into jail without a judge nor writing,
F / C Am
For robbing Colonel Pepper up on Kilgary Mountain;
C / Am
But they didn't take me fists, so I knocked the jailer down,
F / C Am
And bid myself adieu to the jail in Sligo town. *Chorus*

C / Am
Now, some gets their delight in the boxing and the bowling,
F / C Am
And some gets their delight in the hurling and the rolling;
C / Am
But I gets my delight from the juice of the barley,
F / C Am
And courting pretty girls in the morning so early. *Chorus*

None Can Love Like an Irishman

Abraham Lincoln fancied this as a suitable party song. It had been published in London by George Routledge in the 1840s in the *Universal Songster, or Museum of Mirth.* Routledge also published *Uncle Tom's Cabin.*

The tur-baned Turk, __ who scorns the world, May strut a-round with his whisk-ers curled; Keep a hun-dred wives un-der lock and key, For no-bod-y else but him-self to see. Yet long may he pray with his Al-co-ran, Be-fore he can love like an I-rish-man, Yet I-rish-man.

The gay Monsieur, a slave no more,
The solemn Don, the soft Signor,
The Dutch Mynheer, so full of pride,
The Russian, Prussian, Swede beside—
They all may do whate'er they can,
But they'll never love like an Irishman.
They all may do whate'er they can,
But they'll never love like an Irishman.

The London folks themselves beguile,
And think they please in a capital style;
Yet let them ask, as they cross the street,
Of any young virgin they happen to meet,
And I know she'll say, from behind her fan,
That there's none can love like an Irishman.
And I know she'll say, from behind her fan,
That there's none can love like an Irishman.

5

The Next Market Day

A— maid went to Dub - lin her mar – kets to learn, To
sell for her mam - my three hanks of fine yarn,_____ She—
met a young man on the king's own high - way,_____ Which—
caused this young dam - sel to dal - ly and **stray.**

| Dm | | A7 | Dm | | Dm | | A7 | Dm |
Come sit down beside me, I mean you no harm,

She sat down beside him, the grass was so green,
| F | | C7 | F |
Come sit down beside me this new tune to learn,

The day was the fairest that ever was seen,
| Dm | Am | G | A |
Here are three guineas, your mammy to pay,

The look in your eye beats a morning in May,
| Dm | | A7 | Dm |
So leave off your yarning till the next market day.

I could sit by your side till the next market day.

Dm / A7 / Dm
Now as she went homeward, the words he had said,
F / C7 / F
And the tune that he sung her still rung in her head,
Dm / Am / G / A
I'll search for that lad be it land or by sea,
Dm / A7 / Dm
Till he learns me the tune to "The Next Market Day."

Erin Go Bragh

" 'Erin Go Bragh' means 'Ireland forever,' but it was a man's nickname. This poor man was a Scotsman mistaken for an Irishman. These were days when they didn't want Irish in Scotland. It was hard times for Scottish people at home to get work, and they didn't want the poor Irish comin' in. *Erin Go Bragh* dates back to Napoleon's time. I date songs from before Napoleon's time old songs, and from after Napoleon's time pretty new. So as I ken, it's a new song." (Norman Kennedy, Scottish weaver and folk singer interviewed in *Sing out,* Vol. 27, No. 6, 1979)

Dm
My name's Duncan Campell,
    A7   Dm
From the shire of Argyle.
F
I've travelled this country
   C7   F
For many's the mile.
Dm   Am
I've travelled through England
G   A
And Ireland and all;
Dm
But the name I go under's
A7   Dm
Bold Erin Go Bragh.

Dm
One night in auld Rickey,
   A7   Dm
As I walked down the street,
F
A saucy policeman
   C7   F
By chance I did meet.
Dm   Am
He glowered in my face
     G   A
And he gave me some jaw,
Dm
Saying, "When came ye over,
   A7   Dm
Bold Erin Go Bragh?"

Dm
Oh, I'm not a paddy,
      A7   Dm
Though in Ireland I've been.
F
Nor am I a paddy,
     C7   F
Though Ireland I've seen.
Dm   Am
And if I was a paddy,
    G   A
Sure what's that at a'?
Dm
For there's many the bold hero
A7   Dm
From Erin Go Bragh.

```
       Dm                   A7        Dm                          Dm                   A7          Dm
Now I know you're a Pat by the cut of your hair,          Well the people come 'round like a flock of wild geese,
       F             C7              F                              F                   C7            F
But ye's all turned to Scotsmen as soon's you get here.   Crying stop, stop the rascal, he's killed the police,
       Dm       Am      G     A                                    Dm       Am      G      A
Ye've left your own country for breaking the law;         For every friend I had I'm sure he had twa,
       Dm              A7        Dm                                Dm              A7          Dm
We are seizing all stragglers from Erin Go Bragh.         It was very hard times then for Erin Go Bragh.


       Dm                   A7        Dm                          Dm                   A7          Dm
Now if I was a paddy and ye knew it to be true,          So I picked up my all and I headed for the north,
       F             C7              F                              F                   C7            F
If I was a paddy sure what's that to you,                I sailed on a wee boat that crosses the Forth,
       Dm       Am      G     A                                    Dm       Am      G      A
If it wasn't for the baton you hold in your paw,         Farewell to auld Rickey, policemen and a',
       Dm              A7        Dm                                Dm              A7          Dm
I would show you a game played in Erin Go Bragh.         May the devil 'bide with 'em, says Erin Go Bragh.


       Dm                   A7        Dm                          Dm                   A7          Dm
Then a switch of black thorn that I held in my fist,     So come all ye young lads that listen to my song,
       F             C7              F                              F                   C7            F
About his big body I gave it a twist,                    I don't give a farthing to where ye belong
       Dm       Am      G       A A                                Dm       Am      G         A
And the bleed from his napper I soon caused to flow.     My home's in Argyle and the Highland so braw,
       Dm              A7        Dm                                Dm              A7          Dm
I paid him stock and interest from Erin Go Bragh.        But'll ne'er take it ill when called Erin Go Bragh.
```

napper – head
auld Ricky – Edinborough
braw – pretty

Dublin City

As I was a-walkin' thru Dublin City, About the hour of twelve at night. 'Twas there I saw a fair pretty maid —— Washin' her feet by candle light.

```
                            E              C♯m
Chorus:  She had twenty, eighteen, sixteen, fourteen,
                    E                    C♯m
         Twelve, ten eight, six, four two, none.
                        A              F♯m
         She had nineteen, seventeen, fifteen, thirteen,
         G♯7                    C♯m
         Eleven, nine seven, five three and one.
```

```
E                           C♯m                      E                         C♯m
First she wash'd them, and then she dried them,      'Round, 'round the wheel of fortune,
E                           C♯m                      E                         C♯m
'Round her shoulders she pegg'd a towel.             Where it stops wearies me.
      A             F♯m                                    A             F♯m
And in all me life I ne'er did see,                  Fair maids they are so deceivin',
      G♯7               C♯m                                G♯7               C♯m
Such a fine young girl  upon my soul. Chorus         Sad experience teaches me. Chorus
```

I Know My Love

I know my love by his way o' walk in' And I
know my love by his way o' talk - in' And I know my love in a
suit of blue, And if my love leaves me, what will I do - o - o? And
Chorus
Still she cried, "I love him the best, And a trou-bled mind, sure, can know no rest" _____ And
still she cried, "Bon-ny boys are few, And if my love leaves me, what will I do?"

B7   E
There is a dance house in Maradyke, *
B7   E
And there my true love goes every night.
B7   E
He takes a strange one upon his knee,
B7   E
And don't you think that vexes me? *Chorus*

B7   E
If my love knew I could wash and wring,
B7   E
If my love knew I could weave and spin,
B7   E
I'd make a coat of all the finest kind,
B7   E
But the want of money leaves me behind. *Chorus*

*Maradyke- a section of Dublin

John Riley

Fair young maid all in the_____ gar - den,_____

_____ Strange young man pass her_____ by. _____

Said, "Fair maid, _____ will you mar - ry_____ me?"

_____ This then sir _____ was_____ her re - ply. _____

Dm   G Dm
"Oh no, kind sir, I cannot marry,
     G Dm
For I've a love who sails the sea.
   F G   Am
He's been gone for these seven years.
  Em Dm   G Dm
Still no man shall marry me."

Dm   G Dm
"What if he's in battle slain?
      G Dm
Or drowned in the deep salt sea?
   F G   Am
What if he's found another love,
 Em Dm   G Dm
And that they both married be?"

Dm   G Dm
"If he's in some battle slain,
      G Dm
I'll die when the moon doth wane.
    F G   Am
If he's drowned in the deep salt sea,
   Em Dm   G Dm
I'll be true to his memory.

Dm   G Dm
"If he's found another love,
       G Dm
And if they both married be,
    F G   Am
Then I wish them happiness,
     Em Dm   G Dm
Where they dwell across the sea."

Dm   G Dm
He picked her up all in his arms,
      G Dm
Kisses gave her, one, two, three.
    F G   Am
"Weep no more, my own true love,
    Em Dm   G Dm
"I'm your long lost John Riley."

A Rich Irish Lady

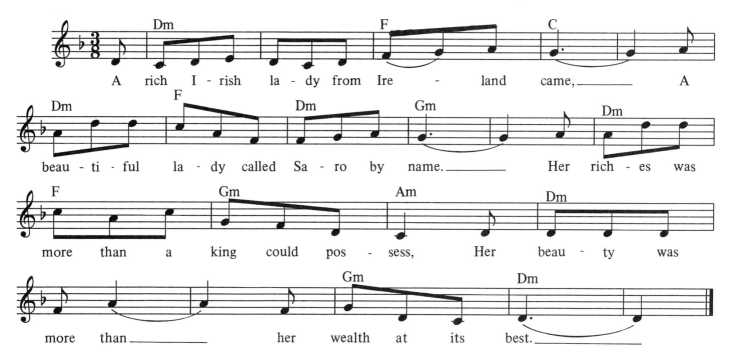

A rich I-rish la-dy from Ire - land came,____ A
beau-ti-ful la-dy called Sa-ro by name.____ Her rich-es was
more than a king could pos-sess, Her beau-ty was
more than ____ her wealth at its best.____

Dm   F C
A lofty young gentleman courtin' her came,
Dm F Dm Gm
Courtin' this lady called Saro by name.
Dm F Gm Am
"O, Saro! O, Saro! O, Saro!" said he,
Dm   Gm Dm
I'm afraid that my ruin forever you'll be.

Dm   F C
"I'm afraid that my ruin forever you'll prove,
Dm F Dm Gm
Unless you turn all of your hatred to love."
Dm F Gm Am
"No hatred to you nor to no other man,
Dm   Gm Dm
But this, for to love you, is more than I can.

Dm   F C
"So, end all your sorrows, and drop your discourse,
Dm F Dm Gm
I never shall have you unless I am forced."
Dm F Gm Am
Six months appeared and five years had passed,
Dm   Gm Dm
When I heard of this lady's misfortune at last.

Dm   F C
She lay wounded by love, and she knew not for why;
Dm F Dm Gm
She sent for this young man whom she had denied.
Dm F Gm Am
And by her bedside these words they were said:
Dm   Gm Dm
"There's pain in your side, love, there's a pain in your head."

Dm   F C
"Oh no, kind sir, the right you've not guessed;
Dm F Dm Gm
The pain that you speak of lies here in my breast."
Dm F Gm Am
"Then am I your doctor, and am I your cure?
Dm   Gm Dm
Am I your protector that you sent for me here?"

Dm   F C
"You are my doctor, and you are my cure;
Dm F Dm Gm
Without your protection I'll die I am sure."
Dm F Gm Am
"O, Saro! O, Saro! O, Saro!" said he,
Dm   Gm Dm
"Don't you remember when I first courted thee?

Dm   F C
"I asked you in kindness, you answered in scorn,
Dm F Dm Gm
I'll never forgive you for times past and gone."
Dm F Gm Am
"Times past and gone I hope you'll forgive,
Dm   Gm Dm
And grant me some longer in comfort to live."

Dm   F C
"I'll never forgive you as long as I live,
Dm   F   Dm Gm
I'll dance on your grave, love, when you're laid in the ground."
Dm F Gm Am
Then off of her fingers gold rings she pulled three,
Dm   Gm   Dm
Saying, "Take them and wear them when you're dancing on me."

Dm   F C
"Adieu, kind friends, adieu all around;
Dm F Dm Gm
Adieu to my true love — God make him a crown;
Dm F Gm Am
I freely forgive him, although he won't me,
Dm   Gm Dm
My follies ten thousand times over I see."

Down by the Sally Gardens

William Butler Yeats (1865–1939), poet, dramatist, and critic, was born near Dublin. He was the first president of the Irish Literary Society and was closely associated with the Abbey Theater, both as director and playwright.

By William Butler Yeats

It was down by the Sal - ly Gar - dens my___ love and ___ I did
passed the ___ Sal - ly Gar - dens on___ lit - tle ___ snow white

meet. She ___ feet. She bid me ___ take love eas - y, As the leaves grow up-on___the ___

tree. But ___ I was ___ young and ___ fool - ish, And with her did - not a - gree.

```
      C  G     F C
In a field by the river,
      F   C G7   C
My love and I did stand.
            G    F    C
And on my leaning shoulder
     F   C  G7      C
She placed her snow-white hand.
   Am Em  F   D7 B7 Em
She bid me take life easy,
       F   Em  Dm7 G7 C
As the grass grows on the weirs.
G7 C7      F    Em  D#° C
But I was young and foolish,
        F  C  G7     C
And now am full of tears.
```

11

The Minstrel Boy

Thomas Moore (1779–1852) was born in Dublin. As a student at Trinity College in Dublin he made the acquaintance of Robert Emmet (cf. page 96). The revolutionary events of 1798 and the execution of Emmet in 1803 made a deep impression on him. His published works date from 1800. In 1807 his publisher suggested to him the task of fitting words to a series of Irish airs. He could not have found an occupation more exactly suited to his powers. The first number of his *Irish Melodies* appeared in 1808. He kept at this project until 1834.

Words by Thomas Moore
Music: The Moreen

The min - strel boy___ to the war is gone, in the ranks of death___ you'll find ___ him. His fa - ther's sword _ he has gird - ed on and his wild harp slung ___ be - hind ___ him. "Land of song," said the war- rior bold, "Tho' all the world be - trays ___ thee, one sword at least___ thy___ rights shall guard, one - faith - ful harp___ shall praise ___ thee.

```
     D                    A    D          G     D           Em7 A7 D
The minstrel fell but the foeman's chain could not bring his proud soul un - der;
     D                A Bm      G      D         Em7 A7 D
The harp he loved ne'er spoke again, for he tore its chords a sun - der.
   Bm  F#7 Bm        A E7 A    F# Bm        F#   Bm
And said "No chains shall sully thee, thou soul of love and bravery!
   G  D                A7    D  F#7    G   D    Em7 A7 D
"Thy songs were made for the pure and free, they shall never sound in sla - very!"
```

Cockles and Mussels

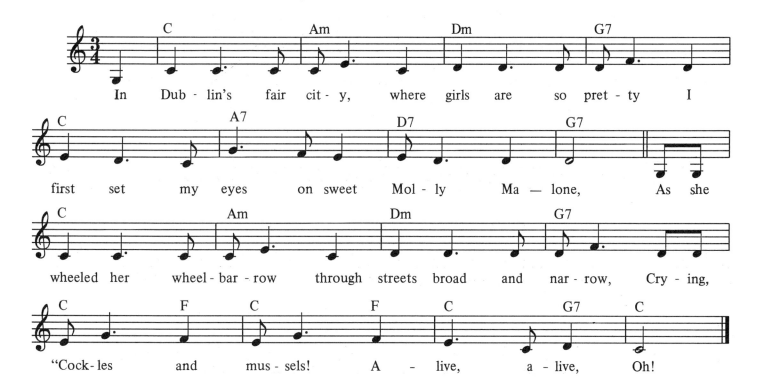

In Dub - lin's fair cit - y, where girls are so pret - ty I

first set my eyes on sweet Mol - ly Ma — lone, As she

wheeled her wheel - bar - row through streets broad and nar - row, Cry - ing,

"Cock - les and mus - sels! A — live, a - live, Oh!

Chorus: *sung to last 8 bars of verse*
C   Am   Dm   G7
Alive, alive-o, alive, alive-o,
           C   F   C   F C   G7 C
Crying "Cockles and mussels alive, alive-o!"

           C   Am   Dm   G7
She was a fishmonger, but sure 'twas no wonder,
           C   A7   D7   G7
For so were her father and mother before.
                 C   Am   Dm   G7
And they each pushed their wheelbarrow through streets broad and narrow,
           C   F   C   FC   G7 C
Crying, "Cockles and mussels! Alive, alive, oh!" *Chorus*

           C   Am   Dm   G7
She died of a "faver," and no one could save her,
           C   A7   D7   G7
And that was the end of sweet Molly Malone;
           C   Am   Dm   G7
Her ghost wheels her barrow through streets broad and narrow,
           C   F   C   FC   G7 C
Crying, "Cockles and mussels! Alive, alive, oh!" *Chorus*

Old Rosin, the Beau

"The humor of exploding many things under the name of trifles, fopperies, and only imaginary goods, is a very false proof either of wisdom or magnanimity, and a great check to virtuous actions. For instance, with regard to fame; there is in most people a reluctance and unwillingness to be forgotten. We observe even among the vulgar, how fond they are to have an inscription over their grave. It requires but little philosophy to discover and observe that there is no intrinsic value in all this; however, if it be founded in our nature, as an incitement to virtue, it ought not to be ridiculed." (Jonathan Swift, 1706)

I live for the good of my na-tion, And my sons are all grow-ing low,___ But I hope the next gen - e - ra - tion Will re - sem-ble old Ros - in, the Beau.___ Re - sem - ble old Ros - in, the Beau,___ Re - sem-ble old Ros - in, the Beau.___ I hope that the next gen - e - ra - tion Will re - sem - ble old Ros - in, the Beau.___

D	G
I've traveled this country all over,	
D	Bm
And now to the next I will go,	
D	G
For I know that good quarters await me	
D A7 D	
To welcome Old Rosin, the Beau.	
G	
To welcome Old Rosin, the Beau,	
D Bm	
To welcome Old Rosin, the Beau,	
D	G
For I know that good quarters await me,	
D A7 D	
To welcome Old Rosin, the Beau.	

D ... G
When I'm dead and laid out on the counter,
D ... Bm
The people all making a show,
D ... G
Just sprinkle plain whisky and water
D A7 D
On the corpse of Old Rosin, the Beau.
G
On the corpse of Old Rosin, the Beau,
D Bm
On the corpse of Old Rosin, the Beau.
D G
Just sprinkle plain whisky and water
D A7 D
On the corpse of Old Rosin, the Beau.

D ... G
In the gay round of pleasures I've traveled.
D ... Bm
Nor will I leave behind a foe.
D ... G
And when my companions are jovial,
D A7 D
They will drink to Old Rosin, the Beau.
G
They will drink to Old Rosin, the Beau,
D Bm
They will drink to Old Rosin, the Beau,
D G
And when my companions are jovial,
D A7 D
They will drink to Old Rosin, the Beau.

D ... G
Then pick me out six trusty fellows,
D ... Bm
And let them stand all in a row,
D ... G
And dig a big hole in the meadow,
D A7 D
And in it toss Rosin, the Beau.
G
And in it toss Rosin, the Beau,
D Bm
And in it toss Rosin, the Beau.
D G
And dig a big hole in the meadow
D A7 D
And in it toss Rosin, the Beau.

D ... G
But my life is now drawn to a closing,
D ... Bm
As all will at last be so.
D ... G
So we'll take a full bumper at parting
D A7 D
To the name of Old Rosin, the Beau.
G
To the name of Old Rosin, the Beau,
D Bm
To the name of Old Rosin, the Beau.
D G
So we'll take a full bumper at parting
D A7 D
To the name of Old Rosin, the Beau.

D ... G
Then bring out two little brown jugs:
D ... Bm
Place one at my head and my toe:
D G
And do not forget to scratch on them
D A7 D
The name of Old Rosin, the Beau.
G
The name of Old Rosin, the Beau,
D Bm
The name of Old Rosin, the Beau.
D G
And do not forget to scratch on them
D A7 D
The name of Old Rosin, the Beau.

Abdullah Bulbul Ameer

William Percy French (1854–1920) was born near Roscommon, at his family residence in Cloonyquin House. He entered Trinity College in 1872 where, as he put it: "I think taking up the banjo, lawn tennis and water color painting, instead of chemistry, geology and the theory of strains retarded my progress a good deal." It was at Trinity that he wrote "Abdullah Bulbul Ameer," which was a great success and has remained a "college song" to this day. After graduation, he worked for some years as an engineer, but continued writing humorous songs.

By Percy French

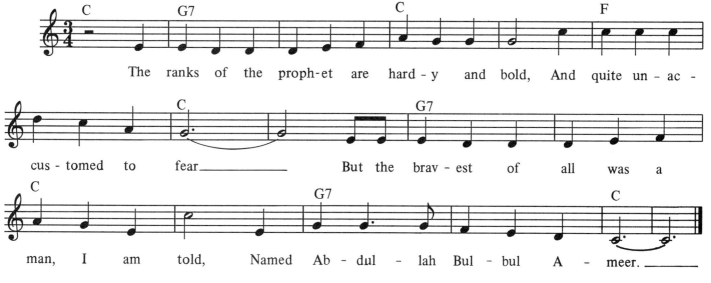

The ranks of the proph-et are hard-y and bold, And quite un-ac-cus-tomed to fear_____ But the brav-est of all was a man, I am told, Named Ab-dul-lah Bul-bul A-meer._____

G7   C
When they needed a man to encourage the van,
F   C
Or to harass a foe from the rear,
G7   C
Storm fort or redoubt, they had only to shout
G7   C
For Abdullah Bulbul Ameer.

G7   C
Now the heroes were plenty and well known to fame,
F   C
Who fought in the ranks of the Czar;
G7   C
But the bravest of these was a man by the name
G7   C
Of Ivan Skavinsky Skivar.

G7   C
He could imitate Pushkin, play poker and pool,
F   C
And strum on the Spanish guitar;
G7   C
In fact, quite the cream of the Muscovite team,
G7   C
Was Ivan Skavinsky Skivar.

G7   C
One day this bold Russian had shouldered his gun,
F   C
And donned his most truculent sneer;
G7   C
Downtown he did go, where he trod on the toe
G7   C
Of Abdullah Bulbul Ameer."

G7   C
"Young man," quoth Bulbul, "has your life grown so dull
F   C
That you're anxious to end your career?
G7   C
Vile infidel, know, you have trod on the toe
G7   C
Of Abdullah Bulbul Ameer."

G7   C
Said Ivan, "My friend, your remarks in the end
F   C
Will avail you but little, I fear:
G7   C
For you ne'er will survive to repeat them alive,
G7   C
Mr. Abdullah Bulbul Ameer."

G7   C
They fought all that night, 'neath the pale yellow moon,
F   C
The din, it was heard from afar,
G7   C
And huge multitudes came, so great was the fame
G7   C
Of Abdul and Ivan Skivar.

G7   C
As Abdul's long knife was extracting the life,
F   C
In fact he had shouted, "Huzzah",
G7   C
He felt himself struck by that wily Calmuck,
G7   C
Count Ivan Skavinsky Skivar.

G7   C
There's a tomb rises up where the Blue Danube rolls,
F   C
And 'graved there in characters clear,
G7   C
Are, "Stranger, when passing, oh, pray for the soul
G7   C
Of Abdullah Bulbul Ameer.

G7   C
A Muscovite maiden, her lone vigil keeps
F   C
'Neath the light of the pale polar star,
G7   C
And the name that she murmurs so oft' as she weeps,
G7   C
Is Ivan Skavinsky Skivar.

Phil the Fluther's Ball

There was, in fact, a Phil the Fluther, who lived in Leitrim and did hold musical rent parties when times got hard.

By Percy French

Have you heard of Phil the Flu-ther, of the town of Bal-ly-muck?__ the
Chorus toot of the flute, and the twid-dle of the fid-dle o,__

times were go-ing hard with him in fact the man was broke, So he just sent out a no-tice to his
hop-ping in the mid-dle like a her-ring on a grid-dle-o,__ Up,-down hands a-roun',

neigh-bours one and all, As__ to how he'd like their com-pan y That eve-ning at a, ball, And__
cross-ing to the wall, Oh,__ had-n't we the gai-e-ty at Phil the Flu-ther's ball.

when writ-in' out, he was care-ful to sug-gest to them, That if they found a hat of his "con-

van-ient to the dure," The more they put in when ev-er he re-quest-ed them, The

bet-ter would the mus-ic be fot bat-ther-in' the floor. With the

(to chorus)

1. There was Mister Denis Dogherty, who kep' the runnin' dog;
 There was little crooked Paddy, from the Tiraloughett bog;
 There was boys from every Barony, and girls from ev'ry "art"
 And the beautiful Miss Bradys in a private ass an' cart.
 And along with them came bouncing Mrs. Cafferty,
 Little Micky Mulligan was also to the fore,
 Rose, Suzanne, and Margaret O'Rafferty
 The flower of Ardmagullion, and the pride of Pethravore. *Chorus*

2. First, little Micky Mulligan got up to show them how,
 And then the Widda' Cafferty steps out and makes her bow,
 I could dance you off your legs, sez she, as sure as, you are born,
 If ye'll only make the piper play, "The Hare Was In The Corn."
 So Phil plays up to the best of his ability,
 The lady and the gentleman begin to do their share;
 Faith then Mick it's you that has agility:
 Begorra Mrs. Cafferty, yer leppin' like a hare! *Chorus*

3. Then Phil the Fluther tipped a wink to little Crooked Pat,
 I think it's nearly time, sez he, for passin' round the hat.
 So Paddy pass'd the caubeen round and looking mighty cute
 Sez, "Ye've got to, pay the piper when he toothers on the flute"
 Then all joined in wid the greatest joviality,,
 Covering the buckle, and the shuffle, and the cut;
 Jigs were danced, of the very finest quality,
 But the widda' bet the company at "handling the fut." *Chorus*

16

Mountains of Mourne

There is a monument at Newcastle, in County Down, under the shadow of the Mourne Mountains — dedicated to Percy French and his song.

By Percy French

Lyrics under music:

Oh Ma-ry, this Lon-don's a won-der-ful sight With the
don't plant po-ta-toes nor bar-ley nor wheat, But there's
all that I found there, I might as well be Where the

peo-ple-all work-ing by day and by night. They
gangs of them dig-ging for gold in the street.
Moun-tains of Mourne sweep down to the sea.

street. At least when I asked them, that's what I was

told, so I just took a hand at that dig-ging for gold; But for

G   C
I believe that when writin', a wish you expressed,
D7   G
As to how the fine ladies in London was dressed;
            C
Now, if you'll believe me, when asked to a ball,
D7   G
Faith, they don't wear no tops to their dresses at all.
D7   G
I've seen them myself, and I would not in troth
       E7   A7   D7
Tell if they was bound for a ball or the bath,
G   C
Don't be startin' them fashions now, Mary McCree,
      D7   G
Where the Mountains of Mourne sweep down to the sea.

G   C
Such beautiful creatures here, och, never mind,
D7   G
With wonderful shapes nature never designed;
          C
And gorgeous complexions all roses and cream,
      D7   G
But O' Loughlan remarks with regards to them same:
      D7   G
That if at those roses you venture to sip,
        E7   A7   D7
The color will all come away on your lip;
      G   B7 *   C   C#dim*
So I'll wait for the wild rose that's waitin' for me
    D7   Gsus4*   G
Where the Mountains of Mourne sweep down to the sea.

* These chords played only here.

Bendemeer's Stream

Words by Thomas Moore

Music: *Mountains of Mourne*

G   C
There's a bower of roses by Bendemeer's stream,
    D7   G
And the nightingale sings 'round it all the day long.
          C
In the time of my childhood 'twas like a sweet dream,
D7   G
To sit in the roses and hear the bird's song.
      D7   G
That bow'r and its music I'll never forget,
         E7   A7   D7
But oft when alone in the bloom of the year,
G   C
I think," Is the nightingale singing there yet?
    D7   G
Are the roses still bright by the calm Bendemeer?"

G   C
No, the roses soon withered that hung o'er the wave,
    D7   G
But some blossoms were gathered while freshly they shone,
          C
And the dew was distilled on the flowers, that gave
    D7   G
All the fragrance of summer - when summer is gone.
      D7   G
Thus memory draws from delight ere it dies,
         E7   A7   D7
An essence that breathes of it many a year.
      G   B7   C   C#dim
Thus, bright to my soul as 'twas then to my eyes
    D7   Gsus4   G
Is that bow'r on the banks of the calm Bendemeer.

Eileen Oge

Words by Percy French
Music: Traditional

Eil - een Oge! an' that the dar-lin's name is. Through the Bar-o-ny her fea-tures they were fa-mous.

If we loved her, who is there to blame us, For__ was-n't she the Pride of Pet-ra-vore?

But her beau-ty made us all so shy, Not a man could look her in the eye.

Boys, O boys! sure that's the rea-son why we're in mourn-in' for the Pride of Pet-ra-vore.

Eil - een Oge! Me heart is grow-in' grey, Ev-er since the day you wan-dered far a-way.

Eil - een Oge! Theres good fish in the say, But theres no one like the Pride of Pet - ra-vore.

1.
Dm   A7   Dm
Friday at the fair of Ballintubber,
C   G7   C
Eileen met McGrath the cattle jobber.
Dm   A7   Dm
I'd like to set me mark upon the robber,
A7   Dm
For he stole away the Pride of Petravore.
Bb   F
He never seemed to see the girl at all.
A7   Dm
Even when she ogled him underneath her shawl.
Bb   F
Lookin' big and masterful when she was lookin' small
Dm   A7   Dm
Most provokin' for the Pride of Petravore. *Chorus*

2.
Dm   A7   Dm
So it went as 'twas in the beginning,
C   G7   C
Eileen Oge she was bent upon the winning.
Dm   A7   Dm
Big McGrath contentedly was grinning,
A7   Dm
Being courted by the Pride of Petravore.
Bb   F
Sez he, "I know a girl that could knock you into fits."
A7   Dm
At that Eileen nearly lost her wits.
Bb   F
The upshot of the ruction was that now the robber sits.
Dm   A7   Dm
With his arm around the Pride of Petravore. *Chorus*

3.
Dm   A7   Dm
Boys. O boys! with fate 'tis hard to grapple.
C   G7   C
Of his eye 'tis Eileen was the apple;
Dm   A7   Dm
And now to see her walkin' to the chapel
A7   Dm
Wid the hardest featured man in Petravore.
Bb   F
And now, boys, this is all I have to say:
A7   Dm
When you do your courtin' don't make a display.
Bb   F
If you want them to run after you, just walk the other way,
Dm   A7   Dm
For they're mostly like the Pride of Petravore. *Chorus*

Real Old Mountain Dew

Sixteenth-century English visitors to Ireland did not think too highly of the "uncivilized" Irish people. However, they did admit that the Irish were a remarkably good-looking people who excelled in nimbleness and flexibility. They were undeniably brave and hardy. But, above all, they made a heavenly drink called "usquebaugh" (*uisce beatha,* "the water of life"), or whisky.

Let grass - es grow, and wa - ters flow, In a free and eas - y way, But give me e-nough of the fine old stuff that's made near Gal - way Bay. Oh peel - ers all, from Don - e - gal. Gal - way and E - trim too, We'll give them the slip and we'll take a sip of the real old Moun - tain Dew.

E	A
At the foot of the hill there's a neat little still,
E	B7
Where the smoke curls up to the sky.
E	A
By the smoke and the smell you can plainly tell
E	B7	E
That there's whisky brewing nearby.

For it fills the air with odor rare,
| C#m B7 |
And betwixt both me and you,
| E | A |
When home you roll you can take a bowl
| E | B7 | E |
Or a bucket of the Mountain Dew.

| E | A |
Now learned men who use the pen,
| E | B7 |
Who've wrote your praises high,
| E | A |
This sweet 'pocheen' from Ireland's green,
| E | B7 | E |
Distilled from wheat and rye.

Throw away your pills, it'll cure all ills
| C#m B7 |
Of pagan or Christian, Jew.
| E | A |
Take off your coat and free your throat
| E | B7 | E |
With the real old Mountain Dew.

Pocheen–potion, i.e., whisky

The Jug of Punch

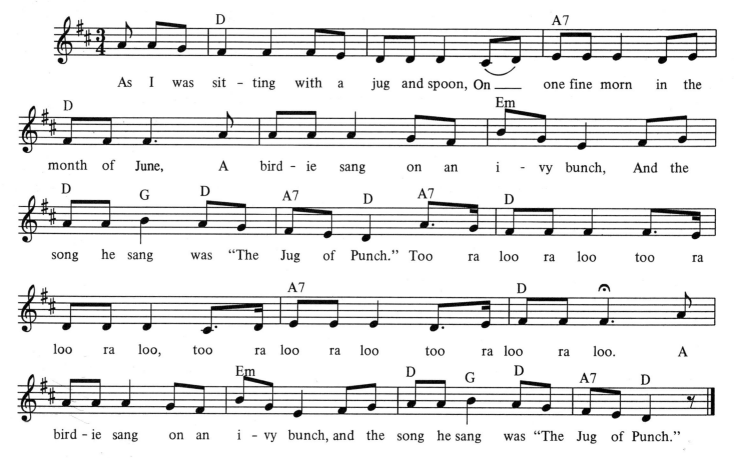

As I was sit-ting with a jug and spoon, On ___ one fine morn in the month of June, A bird-ie sang on an i-vy bunch, And the song he sang was "The Jug of Punch." Too ra loo ra loo too ra loo ra loo, too ra loo ra loo too ra loo ra loo. A bird-ie sang on an i-vy bunch, and the song he sang was "The Jug of Punch."

D
What more diversion can a man desire?
A7   D
Than to court a girl by a neat turf fire?
Em
A Kerry pippin and the crack and crunch,
D   G D A7   D
And on the table a jug of punch.
A7   D
Too ra loo ra loo, too ra loo ra loo,
A7   D
Too ra loo ra loo, too ra loo ra loo,
Em
A Kerry pippin and the crack and crunch,
D   G D A7 D
And on the table a jug of punch.

D
All ye mortal lords drink your nectar wine,
A7   D
And the quality folks drink their claret fine,
Em
I'll give them all the grapes in the bunch
D G D   A7   D
For a jolly pull at the jug of punch.
A7   D
Too ra loo ra loo, too ra loo ra loo,
A7   D
Too ra loo ra loo, too ra loo ra loo,
Em
I'll give them all the grapes in the bunch,
D G D   A7   D
For a jolly pull at the jug of punch.

D
Oh! but when I'm dead and in my grave,
A7   D
No costly tombstone I will crave,
Em
Just lay me down in my native peat,
D   G D   A7   D
With a jug of punch at my head and feet.
A7   D
Too ra loo ra loo, too ra loo ra loo,
A7   D
Too ra loo ra loo, too ra loo ra loo,
Em
Just lay me down in my native peat,
D   G D   A7   D
With a jug of punch at my head and feet.

The Son of a Gambolier

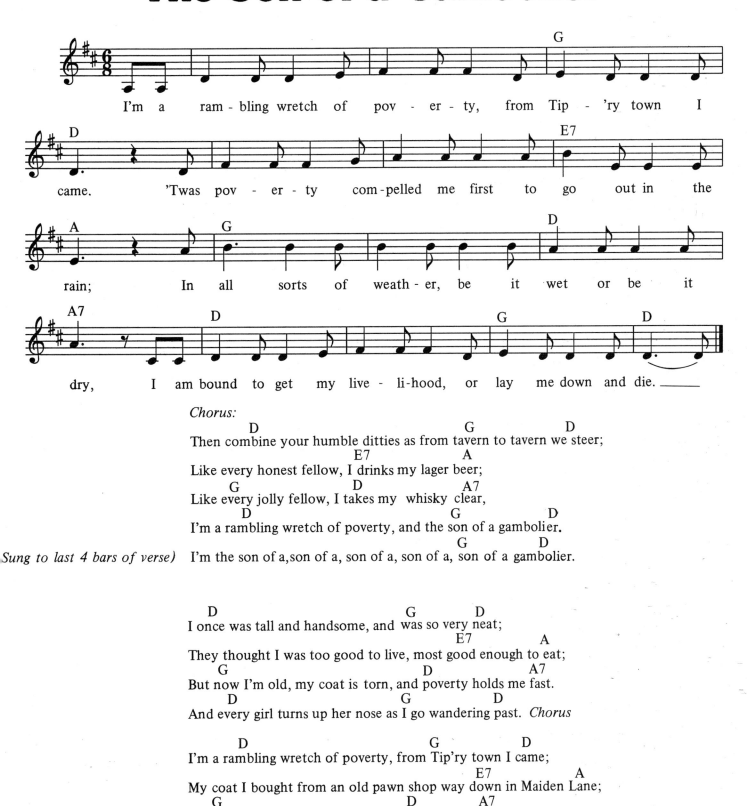

I'm a ram-bling wretch of pov-er-ty, from Tip-'ry town I came. 'Twas pov-er-ty com-pelled me first to go out in the rain; In all sorts of weath-er, be it wet or be it dry, I am bound to get my live-li-hood, or lay me down and die. _____

Chorus:

    D   G   D
Then combine your humble ditties as from tavern to tavern we steer;
                                E7   A
Like every honest fellow, I drinks my lager beer;
    G   D   A7
Like every jolly fellow, I takes my whisky clear,
                D   G   D
I'm a rambling wretch of poverty, and the son of a gambolier.
                                          G   D
Sung to last 4 bars of verse) I'm the son of a, son of a, son of a, son of a, son of a gambolier.

    D   G   D
I once was tall and handsome, and was so very neat;
                                  E7   A
They thought I was too good to live, most good enough to eat;
    G   D   A7
But now I'm old, my coat is torn, and poverty holds me fast.
    D   G   D
And every girl turns up her nose as I go wandering past. *Chorus*

    D   G   D
I'm a rambling wretch of poverty, from Tip'ry town I came;
                                  E7   A
My coat I bought from an old pawn shop way down in Maiden Lane;
    G   D   A7
My hat I got from a sailor lad just eighteen years ago,
                D   G   D
And my shoes I picked from an old dust heap, I'd have you all to know. *Chorus*

Dick Darby

Oh me name is Dick Dar - by, I'm a cob - bler, I ser - ved me time at old camp. Some call me an old ag - i - ta - tor, But now I'm re - solved to re - pent. With me ing - twing of an ing - thing of an i - day, With me ing - twing of an - ing - thing of an i - day, With me roo - boo - boo - roo - boo - boo ran - dy, And me lab stone keeps beat - ing a - way.

      D   A7   D
Now my father was hung for sheep stealing,
                         C
Me mother was burned for a witch,
      D   G   D
My sister's a dandy housekeeper,
        A7   D
And I'm a mechanical switch. *Chorus*

        D   A7   D
Ah, it's forty long years I have traveled,
                         C
All by the contents of me pack,
      D   G   D
Me hammers, me awls and me pinches,
        A7   D
I carry them all on me back. *Chorus*

        D   A7   D
Oh, my wife she is humpy, she's lumpy.
                         C
My wife she's the devil, she's black,
      D   G   D
And no matter what I may do with her,
        A7   D
Her tongue it goes clickety-clack. *Chorus*

        D   A7   D
It was early one fine summer's morning,
                         C
A little before it was day,
      D   G   D
I dipped her three times in the river,
        A7   D
And carelessly bade her "Good day!" *Chorus*

Johnny, I Hardly Knew You

Herbert Hughes, writing in his *Irish Country Songs* (London, 1934), puts it this way: "Johnny . . . is a classic case of a song surviving its period and presenting a problem for the later folklorist." His father, whose memories went back to the American Civil War, felt that it belonged to that period and came from the States — having probably been in the repertory of the Christy Minstrels. It had been published in London in 1867, but internal evidence dates it back perhaps to as early as 1802, when Irish regiments were extensively recruited for the East India service. Whatever its age, its stark message is timeless.

Chorus

Dm   Am
With your guns and drums and drums and guns, huroo, huroo,
Dm   F   A7
With your guns and drums and drums and guns, huroo, huroo,
Dm   C   Dm   A7sus4 A7
With your guns and drums and drums and guns the enemy nearly slew you.
        D   C   Bb   A   Dm   C   Dm
O, my darling dear you look so queer, och, Johnny, I hardly knew you.

Dm   Am
Where are your legs that used to run, huroo, huroo?
Dm   F   A7
Where are your legs that used to run, huroo, huroo?
Dm   C   Dm   A7sus4
Where are your legs that used to run, when first you went to carry
A7
a gun?
Dm   C   Bb   A   Dm   C   Dm
I fear your dancing days are done, och, Johnny, I hardly knew you.
Chorus

Dm   Am
Where are your eyes that were so mild, huroo, huroo?
Dm   F   A7
Where are your eyes that were so mild, huroo, huroo?
Dm   C   Dm   A7sus4
Where are your eyes that were so mild when my heart you so
A7
beguiled?
Dm   C   Bb   A   Dm   C   Dm
Why did you run from me and the child, och, Johnny, I hardly knew you. *Chorus*

Dm   Am
I'm happy for to see you home, huroo, huroo,
Dm   F   A7
I'm happy for to see you home, huroo, huroo,
Dm   C   Dm   A7sus4   A7
I'm happy for to see you home all from the island of   Ceylon,
Dm   C   Bb   A   Dm   C   Dm
So low in flesh, so high in bone, och, Johnny, I hardly knew you.
Chorus

Dm   Am
You haven't an arm and you haven't a leg, huroo, huroo
Dm   F   A7
You haven't an arm and you haven't a leg, huroo, huroo,
Dm   C   Dm
You haven't an arm and you haven't a leg, you're an eyeless,
            A7sus4   A7
boneless, chickenless egg.
Dm   C   Bb   A   Dm   C   Dm
You'll have to be put in a basket to beg, och, Johnny, I hardly knew you. *Chorus*

Missus McGrath

"Oh, Mis-sus Mc-Grath," the ser-geant said, "Would you like to make a sol-dier out of

your son Ted? With a scar-let coat and a big cocked hat; Now

Mis-sus Mc-Grath, would-n't you like that?" *Chorus* Wid yer too-ri-aa,

fol-the-did-dle-aa, Too-ri-oo-ri___ oo-ri-aa. Wid yer

too-ri-aa, fol-the-did-dle-aa. Too-ri-oo-ri-oo-ri-aa.

 G   D7
So Missus McGrath lived on the seashore
        G
For the space of seven long years or more.
              D7   G   D7
Till she saw a big ship sailing into the bay,
     G   D7   G
"Hullaloo, bubaloo, and I think it is he!" *Chorus*

       G   D7
"Oh, Captain dear, where have ye been?
       G
Have you been sailing on the Mediterreen?
               D7   G   D7
Or have you any tidings of my son Ted?
       G   D7 G
Is the poor boy living or is he dead?" *Chorus*

           G   D7
Then up comes Ted without any legs,
         G
And in their place two wooden pegs.
                  D7   G   D7
She kissed him a dozen times or two,
         G   D7   G
Saying, "Holy Moses, 'tisn't you." *Chorus*

          G   D7
"Oh then were ye drunk or were ye blind,
         G
That ye left yer two fine legs behind?
           D7   G   D7
Or was it walking upon the sea
           G   D7   G
Wore yer two fine legs from the knees away?" *Chorus*

       G   D7
"Oh, I wasn't drunk and I wasn't blind
         G
But I left my two fine legs behind;
              D7   G   D7
For a cannon ball on the fifth of May
         G   D7   G
Took my two fine legs from the knees away." *Chorus*

         G   D7
"Oh, then, Teddy me boy, " the widow cried,
         G
"Yer two fine legs were yer mama's pride.
              D7   G   D7
Them stumps of a tree wouldn't do at all,
         G   D7   G
Why didn't ye run from the big cannon ball?" *Chorus*

       G   D7
"All foreign wars I do proclaim,
         G
Between Don John and the King of Spain.
                 D7   G   D7
And by Heavens I'll make them rue the time
         G   D7   G
That they swept the legs from a child of mine." *Chorus*

         G   D7
"Oh, then, if I had ye back again,
         G
I'd never let ye go to fight the King of Spain.
                  D7   G   D7
For I'd rather my Ted as used to be
         G   D7   G
Than the King of France and his whole Navee." *Chorus*

24

Tipperary Recruiting Song

January 7, 1868: A British military force under Sir Robert Napier invades Abyssinia in order to compel King Theodore to release the imprisoned British consul. Once again Irishmen are called upon to die for the Empire. After a short campaign — victory. Prime Minister Disraeli: "He (Napier) led the elephants of Asia, bearing the artillery of Europe, over broken passes which might have startled the trapper of Canada and appalled the hunter of the Alps . . . and we find the standard of St. George hoisted upon the mountains of Rasselas." John Clark Ridpath, writing in his *Life And Times Of Gladstone* (1895), picks up the story: "Thus much for Abyssinia. What of Ireland? In that country things went from bad to worse. There had never been peace. For fully six hundred years of political connection between Ireland and England there had been in the former country only distress, alienation, and the ever-burning spirit of resentment and insurrection. . . . But it is in the character of Great Britain to pursue toward her subject peoples a long course of oppression and spoilation, and then, when her subjects, thus wronged, turn upon her, she calls them rebels, revolutionists, incendiaries and assassins."

'Tis now we'd want to be wa - ry, boys. The re-cruit-ers are out in Tip-pe - ra - ry, boys. If they

of - fer a glass, we'll wink as they pass, We're old birds for chaff in Tip-pe - ra - ry, boys.

G   D
Then, hurrah for the gallant Tipperary boys,
G   D
Although we're 'cross and contrary' boys;
G   G7   C   D7
There's never a one will handle a gun,
Em   D7   G
Except for the Green and Tipperary, boys.

G   D
Now mind what John Bull did here, my boys,
G   D
In the days of our Famine and fear, my boys;
G   G7   C   D7
He burned and sacked, he plundered and racked,
Em   D7   G
Old Ireland of Irish to clear, my boys.

G   D
Now Bull wants to pillage and rob, my boys,
G   D
And put the proceeds in his fob, my boys;
G   G7   C   D7
But let each Irish blade just stick to his trade,
Em   D7   G
And let Bull do his own dirty job, my boys.

G   D
So never to 'list be in haste, my boys,
G   D
Or a glass of drugged whisky to taste, my boys;
G   G7   C   D7
If to India you go, it's to grief and to woe,
Em   D7   G
And to rot and to die like a beast, my boys.

G   D
But now he is beat for men, my boys,
G   D
His army is getting so thin, my boys,
G   G7   C   D7
With the fever and ague, the sword and the plague,
Em   D7   G
O the devil a fear that he'll win, my boys.

G   D
Then mind not the nobblin' old schemer, boys,
G   D
Though he says that he's richer than Damer, boys;
G   G7   C   D7
Though he bully and roar, his power is o'er,
Em   D7   G
And his black heart will shortly be tamer, boys.

G   D
Now, isn't Bull peaceful and civil, boys.
G   D
In his mortal distress and his evil, boys?
G   G7   C   D7
But we'll cock each *caubeen* when his sergeants are seen,
Em   D7   G
And we'll tell them to go to the devil, boys.

G   D
Then hurrah for the gallant Tipperary boys!
G   D
Although 'we're cross and contrary', boys.
G   G7   C   D7
There's never a one will handle a gun,
Em   D7   G
Except for the Green and Tipperary, boys.

caubeen - cap

Damer – John Damer, wealthy 18th-century English nobleman

The Kerry Recruit

Balaklava, Crimea, 25 October 1854: "... As the Russian cavalry moved toward Kadikoi, the 'Heavy Brigade' under General Scarlett charged home with such effect that Menshikov's troops only rallied behind their field near Traktir Bridge. ... The 'Light Brigade' of British cavalry ... now received order to prevent the withdrawal of the guns. ... Lord Cardigan led the Light Brigade straight at the Russian field batteries. ... From the guns in front, on the Fedukhin heights, and on the captured ridge to their right the advancing squadrons at once met a deadly converging fire, but the gallant troopers nevertheless reached the guns and cut down the artillerymen ... but the combat could only end in one way. ... By twos and threes the gallant survivors of the 'Light Brigade' made their way back. Two-thirds of its numbers were left on the field, and the day closed with the Russians still in possession of the Vorontsov ridge." (*Encyclopedia Britannica*, Vol. VII, 1911 edition)

> "... Theirs not to make reply,
> Theirs not to reason why,
> Theirs but to do and die:
> Into the valley of Death
> Rode the six hundred. ..."

("Charge of the Light Brigade," Tennyson)

At the age of nine-teen I was dig-gin' the land with me brogues on me feet and me spade in me hand. Oh says I to me-self, "What a pit-y to see, such a fine Ker-ry lad dig-gin' spuds in Tra-lee." With me Ker-ry-ay-ah, fal lal de ral lay, Ker-ry-ay-ah, fal lal de ral lay.

G	D7	Em
So I buttered me brogues and shook hands with me spade,
A7	D	
And went off to the fair like a dashing young blade.
G	Bm	
A sergeant comes up and says, "Will ye enlist?"
Em	A7	D7
"Sure, Sergeant," says I, "slip the bob in me fist!"   *Chorus*

G	D7	Em
The first thing they gave me it was a red coat,
A7	D	
With a lump of black leather to tie round me throat
G	Bm	
The next thing they gave me, says I, "What is that?"
Em	A7	D7
"Sure, man, a cockade for to stick in yer hat"   *Chorus*

G	D7	Em
Then up steps the captain, a man of great fame,
A7	D	
And straightway he aske me my country and name,
G	Bm	
"I've told ye before, and I tell ye again
| Em | A7 | D7 |
Me father and mother were two Kerry men."   *Chorus*

G	D7	Em
The next thing they gave me they called it a gun,
A7	D	
And under the trigger I settled me thumb.
G	Bm	
The gun it belched fire and vomited smoke,
Em	A7	D
And gave me poor shoulder the devil's own stroke.   *Chorus*

```
        G                           D7        Em
Now the first place they took us was down to the sea,
   A7                      D
Aboard a great ship bound for the Crimee.
            G                      Bm
With three sticks in the middle all hung with white sheets,
   Em                    A7       D7
She walked on the water without any feet.    Chorus
```

```
        G                         D7      Em
The next thing they gave me they called it a horse,
      A7                    D
With saddle and bridle me two legs across.
        G                  Bm
So I gave it the bit and I gave it the steel,
Em                       A7       D7
And Holy Mother! She went like an eel!    Chorus
```

```
        G                D7       Em
We reached Balaklava all safe and all sound,
      A7                 D
And hungry and weary we lay on the ground.
         G                    Bm
Next morning at daybreak a bugle did call,
   Em                     A7       D7
And served us a breakfast of powder and ball. Chorus
```

```
        G                  D7       Em
We licked them at Alma and Innerman,
         A7                    D
But the Russians they foiled us at the Redan.
            G                  Bm
While scaling the ramparts meself lost an eye,
     Em                      A7         D7
And a great Russian bullet ran away with me thigh.    Chorus
```

```
        G                  D7       Em
All bleeding and dying I lay on the ground,
      A7                    D
With arms, legs, and feet all scattered around.
        G                  Bm
Says I to meself, "If me father were nigh,
      Em                  A7         D7
He'd have buried me now just in case I should die!"    Chorus
```

```
        G                       D7       Em
But a surgeon comes by and he soon stops the blood,
      A7                    D
And he gave me an iligant leg made of wood.
              G                Bm
And they made me a pension of ten pence a day,
           Em                A7       D7
And contented with shellocks I live on half pay.    Chorus
```

```
        G                   D7       Em
Now that is the story me grandfather told,
      A7                D
As he sat by the fire all withered and old.
        G                      Bm
"Remember," he says, "that the Irish fight well,
              Em             A7       D7
But the Russian artillery's hotter than Hell!"    Chorus
```

shellocks - shellfish

27

Join the British Army

A barrack-room favorite since Victorian days, this ultimate put-down of (all) military service is also a street ditty of children in Dublin, Belfast, and Glasgow. From the singing of Brendan and Dominic Behan and Ewan McColl, who learned it from his father.

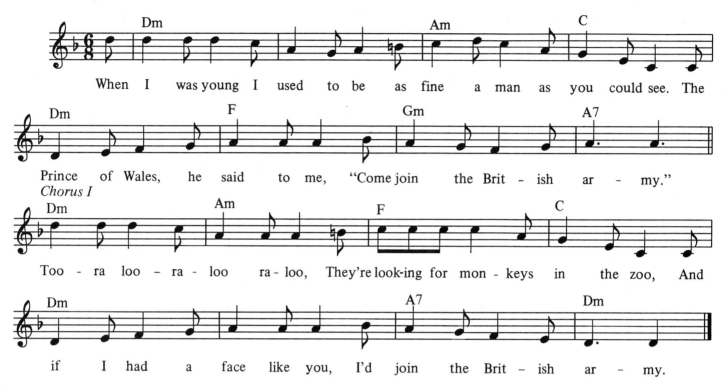

When I was young I used to be as fine a man as you could see. The Prince of Wales, he said to me, "Come join the Brit – ish ar – my."

Chorus I

Too – ra loo – ra – loo ra – loo, They're look-ing for mon – keys in the zoo, And if I had a face like you, I'd join the Brit – ish ar – my.

Dm
Sarah Comden baked a cake,
Am   C
'Twas all for Corporal Slattery's sake.
Dm   F
I threw meself into the lake,
Gm   A7
Pretendin' I was barmy.

              Dm   Am
Chorus: Too ra loo ra loo ra loo,
                 F   C
            'Twas the only thing that I could do
            Dm
            To work me ticket home to you,
            A7   Dm
            And leave the British army.

Dm
Sergeant Daly's gone away,
Am   C
His wife is in the family way.
Dm   F
The only thing that she can say,
Gm   A7
Is, "Blame the British army!"

              Dm   Am
Chorus: Too ra loo ra loo ra loo
                F   C
            Me curses on the Labor crew.
            Dm
            They took your darlin' boy from you
            A7   Dm
            To join the British army.

Dm
Captain Duff's got such a drought,
Am   C
Just give him a couple of jars of stout,
Dm   F
And he'll beat the enemy with his mouth,
Gm   A7
And save the British army.   *Chorus I*

Dm
Kilted soldiers wear no drawers,
Am   C
Won't you kindly lend them yours?
Dm   F
The poor should always help the poor
Gm   A7
God help the British army!   *Chorus I*

Dm
They'll beat the German's without fuss
Am   C
And lay their bones out in the dust.
Dm   F
I know, for they damn' near beat us -
Gm   A7
The gallant British army.

              Dm   Am
Chorus: Too ra loo ra loo ra loo,
                F   C
            I've made me mind up what to do:
            Dm
            I'll work me ticket home to you,
            A7   Dm
            And leave the British army.

                     Repeat first verse and chorus

From Erin's Shores

1603. James I, son of Mary Stuart, accedes to the throne. The English system of land ownership is violently substituted for the old Irish system. The Earl of Tyrone, harassed by sheriffs, leaves Ireland accompanied by Rory O'Connell, Earl of Tyrconnel. The "flight of the earls," as it is called, completes the ruin of the Celtic cause. . . .

Words by Florence Hoare

Melody
"The Flight of the Earls"

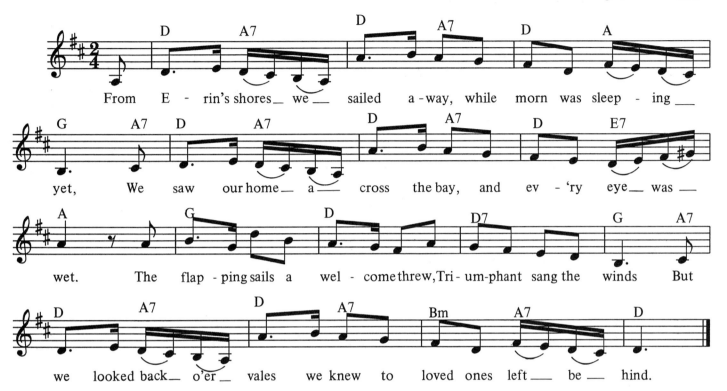

From E - rin's shores___ we___ sailed a -way, while morn was sleep - ing ___

yet, We saw our home___ a___ cross the bay, and ev - 'ry eye___ was ___

wet. The flap - ping sails a wel - come threw, Tri - um-phant sang the winds But

we looked back___ o'er ___ vales we knew to loved ones left ___ be ___ hind.

D	A7	D	A7	

Tho' memory should smiling come
D   A   G
To cheer the distant shore,
A7 D A7   D   A7
The simple joys of hearth and home
D   E7 A
Would be our own no more.
G   D
As some dear face seems fairer grown
D7   G
Beneath a loving eye,
A7 D A7 D   A7
So Erin wore a grace unknown,
Bm   A7   D
The day we said goodbye.

Yet sang the breezes in our ear,
D   A   G
Like beat of martial feet,
A7 D A7   D   A7
And fame to Erin's heart is dear,
D   E7   A
Ambition's paths are sweet.
G   D
And so we turned and sailed away,
D7   G
While morn was sleeping yet,
A7 D A7   D   A7
But Erin's Isle and Erin's smile,
Bm   A7   D
We never shall forget.

The Flying Cloud

The "Guinea trade" — slaving — openly carried on by American ships in the 18th century, was prohibited by several Acts of Congress between 1807 and 1823. This song probably dates from somewhere between 1819 and 1825, when the West Indies were finally cleared of pirates by combined United States and European naval powers. Before this date the Caribbean was infested by slavers turned pirates and pirates turned slavers as the winds changed.

My name is Ar-thur Hol-lan-din, as you may un-der-stand, I was born ten miles from Dub-lin Town, down on the salt-sea strand; When I was young and come-ly, sure, good for-tune on me shone, My par-ents loved me -ten-der-ly, for ___ I was their on-ly son.

A   E7   A
My father he rose up one day and with him I did go,
           E7
He bound me as a butcher's boy to Pearson of Wicklow,
A   E7
I wore the bloody apron there for three long years and more,
  A D A Bm E7   A
Till I shipped on board of *The Ocean Queen* belonging to Tramore.

A   E7   A
It was on Bermuda's Island that I met with Captain Moore,
           E7
The Captain of *The Flying Cloud*, the pride of Baltimore,
A   E7
I undertook to ship with him on a slaving voyage to go,
  A D A Bm E7   A
To the burning shores of Africa, where the sugar cane does grow.

A   E7   A
It all went well until the day we reached old Africa's shore,

And five hundred of them poor slaves, me boys, from their native
          E7
 land we bore,
        A
Each man was loaded down with chains as we made them walk
  E7
 below,
  A   D A Bm E7   A
Just eighteen inches of space was all that each man had to show.

A   E7   A
The plague it came and fever too and killed 'em off like flies,
            E7
We dumped their bodies on the deck and hove 'em overside,
 A
For sure, the dead were the lucky ones for they'd have to weep no
E7
 more,
  A   D A Bm E7   A
Nor drag the chain and feel the lash in slavery for evermore.

```
     A                                      E7            A
But now our money it is all spent, we must go to sea once more,
                                                      E7
And all but five remained to listen to the words of Captain Moore,
       A                                      E7
"There's gold and silver to be had if with me you'll remain,
       A      D      A   Bm       E7            A
Let's hoist the pirate flag aloft and sweep the Spanish Main."

       A                                      E7            A
The Flying Cloud was a Yankee ship, five hundred tons or more,
                                                      E7
She could outsail any clipper ship hailing out of Baltimore,
       A                                              E7
With her canvas white as the driven snow and on it there's no specks,
       A      D      A      Bm       E7            A
And forty men and fourteen guns she carried below her decks.

       A                                      E7            A
We plundered many a gallant ship down on the Spanish Main,
                                                      E7
Killed many a man and left his wife and children to remain,
       A                                              E7
To none we showed no kindness but gave them watery graves,
          A      D      A   Bm       E7            A
For the saying of our captain was: "Dead men tell no tales."

       A                                      E7            A
We ran and fought with many a ship both frigates and liners too,
                                                      E7
Till, at last, a British Man-O'-War, the Dunmow, hove in view,
       A                                      E7
She fired a shot across our bows as we ran before the wind,
          A      D      A      Bm       E7            A
And a chainshot cut our mainmast down and we fell far behind.

       A                              E7            A
They beat our crew to quarters as they drew up alongside,
                                                      E7
And soon across our quarterdeck there ran a crimson tide,
       A                                              E7
We fought until they killed our captain and twenty of our men,
          A      D      A   Bm       E7            A
Then a bombshell set our ship on fire, we had to surrender then.

       A                                      E7            A
It's now to Newgate we have come, bound down with iron chains,
                                                      E7
For the sinking and the plundering of ships on the Spanish Main,
       A                                              E7
The judge he has condemned us and we are condemned to die.
          A      D      A   Bm       E7      A
Young men a warning by me take and shun all piracy.

       A                              E7            A
Farewell to Dublin City and the girl that I adore,
                                                      E7
I'll never kiss your cheek again nor hold your hand no more,
 A                                                    E7
Whisky and bad company have made a wretch of me,
          A      D      A   Bm       E7      A
Young men, a warning by me take and shun all piracy.
```

The Irish Girl

"I had rather be beside her on a couch kissing her ever than be sitting in heaven in the chair of the Trinity." (A young Irishman in love)

As I walked out one eve - ning __ down __ by a __ riv - er side, While gaz - ing all a - round __ me an __ Ir - ish __ girl __ I __ spied; A __ ro - sy red was on her __ cheeks and __ coal - black was __ her __ hair, And __ cost - ly were the robes of __ gold __ this __ Ir - ish __ girl did wear.

```
        A          G       A       E    D     A
The little shoes this maiden wore were of a Spanish brown,
E   A              G     A              E
The mantle on her shoulders of silk 'twas wrought all round;
          A            G      A         E
Her modest face, her gentle ways, have left my heart in pain,
            A                   E  D    A
And I'd range this world all over my Irish girl to gain.

        A        G       A      E      D    A
I wish my love a red, red, rose, to bloom in yon garden fair,
E   A             G        A           E
And I to be the gardener, that rose should be my care.
              A                   G       A         E
And I'd tend the pretty flowers all round, sweet william, pink and rue,
        A                       E     D  A
Primrose and thyme, but most of all, sweet rose, I'd cherish you.

        A            G      A     E       D      A
I wish I was a butterfly, I'd light on my love's breast,
E   A                 G      A            E
I wish I was a nightingale to sing my love to rest;
          A              G      A             E
I'd sing at morn, I'd sing at eve, a love song sweet and slow,
          A                    E      D    A
And year by year I'll love my dear, let the wind blow high or low.
```

The Tanyard Side

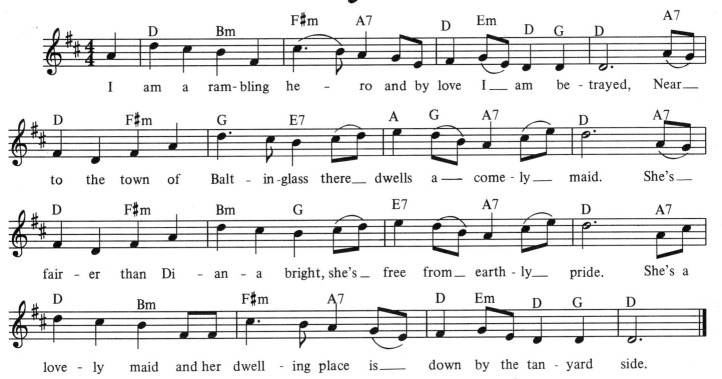

I am a ram-bling he - ro and by love I __ am be - trayed, Near __ to the town of Balt - in -glass there __ dwells a — come - ly __ maid. She's __ fair - er than Di - an - a bright, she's __ free from __ earth - ly __ pride. She's a love - ly maid and her dwell - ing place is __ down by the tan - yard side.

       D   Bm F♯m A7   D Em D G D
I stood in meditation and I viewed her o'er and o'er,
A7 D   F♯m   G   E7   A G   A7   D
I thought she was an angel bright descended down so low.
A7 D   F♯m   Bm   G   E7 A7   D
O no, kind sir, I'm a country girl, she modestly replied,
   A7   D Bm F♯m   A7   D Em D G   D
And I labour daily for my bread down by the tanyard side.

          D   Bm   F♯m A7   D Em D G D
Her golden hair in ringlets rare fell down her snow-white neck.
   A7 D   F♯m G   E7   A G A7   D
The killing glances of her eyes would save a ship from wreck.
   A7   D   F♯m   Bm G   E7   A7 D
Her two brown sparkling eyes and her teeth of ivory white
     A7   D Bm F♯m   A7   D Em D G D
Would make a man become her slave down by the tanyard side.

         D   Bm   F♯m A7   D Em D GD
For twelve long months we courted till at length we did agree
   A7   D   F♯m   G E7   A G A7   D
That we'd acquaint her parents and married we would be.
   A7   D   F♯m Bm G   E7   A7   D
'Twas then her cruel parents to me did prove unkind.
    A7   D   Bm F♯m   A7   D Em D GD
Which makes me sail across the sea and leave my love behind.

         D   Bm F♯m A7   D Em D G D
Farewell, my aged parents, and to you I bid adieu,
   A7 D   F♯m   G E7   A G A7   D
I'm crossing the main ocean all for the sake of you.
   A7   F♯m Bm G   E7   A7   D
And if I e'er return again I'll take you for my bride,
   A7   D   F♯m   A7   D Em G   D
And I'll roll you in my arms, my love, down by the tanyard side.

The Harp That Once

Tara, located in County Meath, is a village whose history dates back to antiquity. Legend has it that in the 9th century, B.C., the Tautha Dé Danaan ("tribes of the god Danu"), having fled Greece because of a Syrian invasion, arrived in Scandinavia. Under Nuadu Airgelaim they moved to Scotland and finally arrived in Ireland around 924 B.C., bringing with them the celebrated Lia Fail ("stone of destiny"), which they set up at Tara. In the time of St. Patrick, Tara is mentioned as the chief seat of druidism and idolatry, and in about 560 A.D. it was abandoned as a royal residence. In 980, Malachy defeated the Ostmen (Danes) of Dublin in battle here and took over the throne of this ancient hill town. As king of Meath he divided Ireland officially between himself and Brian Boru, who ruled in the south as king of Cashel. On May 26, 1798, yet another battle took place in Tara. An attempted rebellion against British rule by the United Irishmen was crushed here and in other regions of the country.

Words, by Thomas Moore

The harp that once thro' Ta - ra's halls its soul of mu - sic shed, Now hangs as mute on Ta - ra's walls as if that soul were fled. So sleeps the pride of for - mer days, so glo - ry's thrill is o'er, And hearts that once beat high for praise now feel that pulse no more.

    C   F
No more to chiefs and ladies bright
    C   G7   C
The harp of Tara swells,
                 G7
The chord alone that breaks at night,
    C   G7
Its tale of ruin tells.
          C   G7
Thus freedom now so seldom wakes;
    C   F
The only throb she gives,
G7 Am   F
Is when some heart indignant breaks,
    C   G7   C
To show that she still lives.

Brennan on the Moor

Willie Brennan was the Irish counterpart of Robin Hood and Jesse James. In the late eighteenth century he held sway in the Kilworth Mountains in County Cork until his execution on the gallows in 1804.

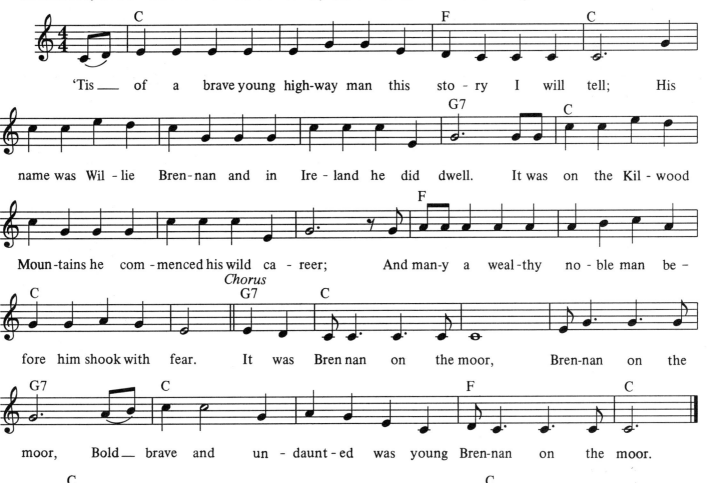

'Tis — of a brave young high-way man this sto - ry I will tell; His name was Wil - lie Bren-nan and in Ire - land he did dwell. It was on the Kil - wood Moun-tains he com - menced his wild ca - reer; And man-y a weal-thy no - ble man be - fore him shook with fear. It was Bren nan on the moor, Bren-nan on the moor, Bold — brave and un - daunt - ed was young Bren-nan on the moor.

C
One day upon the highway,
F   C
As Willie he went down,

He met the Mayor of Cashell
G7
A mile outside the town.
C
The mayor he knew his features,

And he said, "Young man," said he,
F
"Your name is Willie Brennan,
C
You must come along with me." *Chorus*

C
Now Brennan's wife had gone to town,
F   C
Provisions for to buy,

And when she saw her Willie,
G7
She commenced to weep and cry;
C
Said, "Hand to me that tenpenny."

As soon as Willie spoke,
F
She handed him a blunderbuss
C
From underneath her cloak. *Chorus*

C
Now with this loaded blunderbuss,
F   C
The truth I will unfold —

He made the mayor to tremble,
G7
And he robbed him of his gold.
C
One hundred pounds was offered

For his apprehension there,
F
So he, with horse and saddle,
C
To the mountains did repair. *Chorus*

C
Now Brennan being an outlaw
F   C
Upon the mountains high,

With cavalry and infantry,
G7
To take him they did try.
C
He laughed at them with scorn

Until at last, 'twas said,
F
That by a woman false of heart
C
He was cruelly betrayed. *Chorus*

As I Was Going to Ballynure

Country Antrim

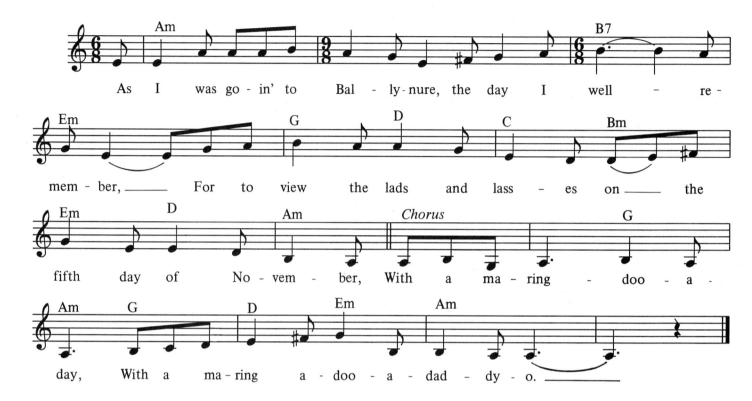

As I was go-in' to Bal-ly-nure, the day I well – re-
mem – ber, _____ For to view the lads and lass – es on _____ the
fifth day of No – vem – ber, With a ma – ring – doo – a –
day, With a ma – ring a – doo – a – dad – dy – o. _____

Am
As I was goin' along the road,
         B7   Em
When homeward I was walking,
  G   D C   Bm
I heard a wee lad behind a ditch,
     Em   D   Am
To his wee lass he was **talking**. *Chorus*

      Am
Said the wee lad to the wee lass,
         B7   Em
"It's will ye let me kiss ye?
      G   D   C   Bm
For it's I have got the cordial eye
      Em D   Am
That far exceeds the whisky." *Chorus*

      Am
This cordial that ye talk about,
          B7   Em
There's very few that gets it,
      G   D   C   Bm
For there's nothin' now but crooked crumbs,
      Em   D   Am
And muslin gowns can catch it.   *Chorus*

She Moved Through the Fair

County Donegal

My____ young love said to me, ____ "My__ moth-er won't mind, And my

fath-er _____ won't slight you for your lack of kind._____ And she

stepped_____ a-way from me and this she did say, "It_____

will not be long, love, _____ till____ our wed-ding day._____

D.   C   D   C   D
She stepped away from me and she went through the fair,
      Am   Bm   C   D
And fondly I watched her move here and move there,
      Am   Bm   C   D
And then she went homeward with one star awake,
      C   D   C   D
As the swan in the evening moves over the lake.

D   C   D   C   D
Last night she came to me, she came softly in.
      Am   Bm   C   D
So softly she came that her feet made no din.
      Am   Bm   C   D
And she laid her hand on me and this she did say,
      C   D   C   D
"It will not be long, love, till our wedding day."

Norah O'Neale

County Derry

Chorus

I'm _____ lone - ly to - night, love, with - out you, _____ And my love I can nev - er con - ceal, For they say there's a charm, love a - bout you, _____ My dar - ling sweet - No-rah o' Neale. *Fine* Like the beam of the star when it's shin - ing, _____ Is the glance which your eye can't con - ceal, And your voice is so sweet and be - guil - ing, _____ That I love you, sweet ___ No-rah o' Neale.

Bm   Em   Bm Em
The nightingale sings in the wild wood,
Bm   E   D B7
As if every note that he knew
E   F#7   B7   E
Was learned from your sweet voice in childhood,
A   B7   E
To remind me, sweet Norah, of you. *Chorus*

The Lowlands of Holland

The "enemy" being fought in the "lowlands of Holland" is probably Spain under Phillip II. England was aiding Protestant Netherlands in their attempt to cast off Spanish Catholic rule in 1587. Things get a bit mixed up in verse three, however, with its references to sugar cane and "fruit on every tree". That sounds like New Holland, which was the original name for Australia.

County Derry

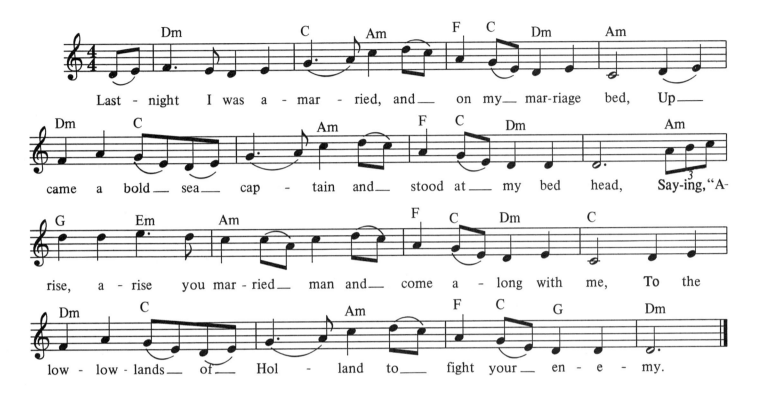

Last-night I was a-mar-ried, and__ on my__ mar-riage bed, Up__ came a bold__ sea__ cap-tain and__ stood at__ my bed head, Say-ing, "A-rise, a-rise you mar-ried__ man and__ come a-long with me, To the low-low-lands__ of__ Hol-land to__ fight your__ en-e-my.

Dm   C   Am
She held her love all in her arms.
F   C Dm   Am
Still thinking he might stay,
Dm   C   Am
When the captain gave another shout,
F   C Dm
He was forced to go away.
Am G   Em   Am
It's many a blithe young married man
F   C   Dm   C
This night must go with me
Dm   Am
To the low, lowlands of Holland,
F   C   G Dm
To fight the enemy.

Dm   C   Am
Oh! Holland is a wondrous place,
F C Dm   Am
And in it grows much green.
Dm   C Am
It's a wild inhabitation
F   C Dm
For my love to be in.
Am   G Em   Am
There the sugar cane grows plentiful,
F   C Dm C
And fruit on every tree,
Dm   Am
But the low, lowlands of Holland
F   C   G   Dm
Are between my love and me.

Dm   C   Am
Nor shoe nor stocking I put on,
F   C   Dm   Am
Nor a comb to go in my hair,
Dm   C Am
And neither coal nor candlelight
F   C Dm
Shine in my chamber fair,
Am G   Em   Am
Nor will I wed with any young man
F C Dm C
Until the day I die,
Dm   C   Am
Since the low, lowlands of Holland
F   C G   Dm
Are between my love and me.

The Star of County Down

Near to Ban-bridge town, in the Coun-ty Down on a morn-ing— in Ju-ly, Down a
bo-reen green came a sweet cai-leen And she smiled as she passed me by. Oh! she
looked so neat, from her two white feet to the sheen of her nut brown— hair Such a
coax-ing elf, I'd to shake my-self to make sure I was real-ly there. Oh! from
Ban-try Bay up to Der-ry Quay, and from Gal-way to Dub-lin— town, No—
maid I've seen like the brown cai-leen that I met in the Coun-ty Down.

Em   A
As she onward sped I scratched my head,
    Em   Bm
And I gazed with a feeling quare,
    Em   A
There I said, said I, to a passer by,
    Em   A   Em
"Who's the maid with the nut - brown hair?"
    G   D
Oh, he smiled at me, and with pride says he,
    Em   Bm
"That's the gem of Ireland's crown,
    Em   A
Young Rosie McCann, from the banks of Bann,
    Em   A   Em
She's the star of County Down." *Chorus*

          Em   A
At the harvest fair she'll surely be there,
      Em   Bm
So I'll dress in my Sunday clothes;
        Em   A
And I'll try sheep's eyes and deludtherin lies
    Em   A   Em
On the heart of the nut - brown Rose.
    G   D
No pipe I'll smoke, no horse I'll yoke,
        Em   Bm
Tho' my plough with rust turn brown,
    Em   A
Till a smiling bride by my own fireside,
          Em   A   Em
Sits the star of County Down. *Chorus*

Shule Agra

During the American Revolutionary War this song was sung as "Johnny Has Gone for a Soldier." *Shule (suil) agra* means "go, my dear." The meaning of the chorus is "May you walk safely, my beloved" — appropriate for both the Irish and American versions.

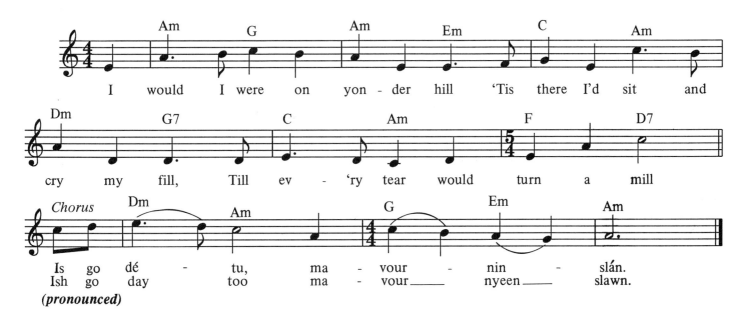

I would I were on yon-der hill 'Tis there I'd sit and cry my fill, Till ev-'ry tear would turn a mill

Chorus

Is go dé - tu, ma - vour - nin - slán.
Ish go day too ma - vour_____ nyeen_____ slawn.
(pronounced)

      Am   G   Am   Em
I'll sell my rack, I'll sell my reel,
        C   Am   Dm   G7
And then I'll sell my spinning wheel,
          C   Am   F   D7
For to buy my love a sword of steel. *Chorus*

      Am   G   Am   Em
I'll dye my petticoat, I'll die it red,
        C   Am   Dm   G7
And 'round the world I'll beg my bread,
  C   Am   F   D7
Until my parents shall wish me dead. *Chorus*

      Am   G   Am   Em
But now my love has gone to France
      C   Am   Dm   G7
To try his fortune to advance,
        C   Am   F   D7
If he ever comes back 'tis but a chance. *Chorus*

Molly Brannigan

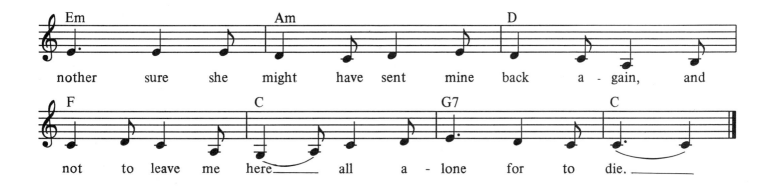

nother   sure   she   might   have   sent   mine   back   a - gain,   and

not   to   leave   me   here_____   all   a - lone   for   to   die. _____

F   Am   Dm   Am
Man, dear, I remember when the milking time was past and
done,
F   C   Dm   Am
We went into the meadows where she swore I was the only
one,
F   Am   Dm   Am
That ever she could love, yet oh, the base, the cruel one,
F   C   G7   C
After that to leave me all alone for to die.
C7   F   C
Man, dear, I remember as we came home the rain began,
F   Am   Dm   Am
I rolled her in my coat though never a waistcoat I had on,
F   Em   Am   D
My shirt was rather fine drawn, yet oh, the base, the cruel one,
F   C   G7   C
After that to leave me all alone for to die.

F   Am   Dm   Am
I went and told my story first to Father Matt McDonnel, man,
F   C   Dm   Am
And then I went and asked advice of Counselor O'Connell,
man,
F   Am   Dm   Am
He said that promise breaches had been ever since the world
began,
F   C   G7   C
Now I have only one pair and they're corduroy.
C7   F   C
Alas, what could he mean man, and what could you advise me
do,
F   Am   Dm   Am
Must my corduroys to Molly go, in troth I'm bothered what
to do,
F   Em   Am   D
I can't afford to lose both my heart and then my britches too,
F   C   G7   C
For what have I left now to do, but only to die.

F   Am   Dm   Am
Oh, the left side of my carcass is as weak as water gruel, man,
F   C   Dm   Am
The devil a bit upon my hide, since Molly's been so cruel, man,
F   Am   Dm   Am
I wish I had a blunderbuss, I'd go and fight a duel, man,
F   C   G7   C
It's better far to kill myself than stay here to die.
C7   F   C
I'm cool and determined as a live salamander, man,
F   Am   Dm   Am
Won't you come to my wake, when I go my long meander, man,
F   Em   Am   D
I'll be feeling just as valiant as the famous Alexander, man,
F   C   G7   C
When I hear you crying 'round me, "Arrah, why did he die?"

Where the Grass Grows Green

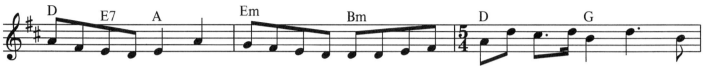

I'm Den-is Doyle from Coun-try Clare, I'm here at your com-mand, To sing a song in praise of home, our

dear old na-tive land. I've sailed to for-eign coun-tries and to ma-ny climes I've been, But my

heart is still with Er-in, where the grass grows green. I love my na-tive coun-try and tho?

rich-er lands I've seen yet I can't for-get old Ire-land where the grass grows green.

```
         D   Em        Bm        Em    A7      D
Poor Paddy's often painted with a ragged coat and hat,
               G              D   E7       A
But his heart and hospitality's a lot to do with that.
        Em        Bm              D        G
Let slanderers say what they will, they cannot call him mean,
        D           A7            D
For a stranger's always welcome where the grass grows green.
           Em        Bm               G
Let slanderers say what they will, they cannot call him mean,
G#dim D              A7              D  G  D
For a stranger's always welcome where the grass grows green.
```

```
   D  Em          Bm          Em      A7      D
It's true he has a weakness for a drop of something pure,
        G                D   E7       A
But that's a slight debility that many more endure.
        Em        Bm          D          G
He's fond of fun, he's witty – tho' his wit is not too keen,
            D           A7            D
For there's tender hearts in Ireland where the grass grows green.
           Em        Bm          D          G
He's fond of fun, he's witty – tho  his wit is not too keen,
G#dim       D          A7              D  G  D
For there's tender hearts in Ireland where the grass grows green.
```

```
   D   Em            Bm          Em      A7      D
There's not a trueborn Irishman, wherever he may be,
        G                D   E7       A
But loves the little emerald that sparkles in the sea.
           Em              Bm          D        G
May the sun of  bright  prosperity shine peaceful and serene,
            D           A7            D
And bring better days to Ireland where the grass grows green.
           Em              Bm          D        G
May the sun of  bright  prosperity shine peaceful and serene,
G#dim       D              A7              D  G  D
And bring better days to Ireland where the grass grows green.
```

Oh, Limerick Is Beautiful

By Michael Scanlan (1836 - 1900)

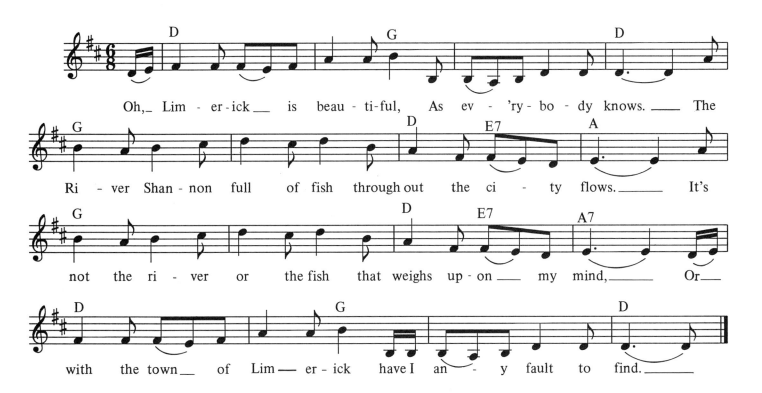

Oh,_ Lim - er - ick_ is beau - ti-ful, As ev - 'ry - bo - dy knows. _ The
Ri - ver Shan - non full of fish through out the ci - ty flows. _ It's
not the ri - ver or the fish that weighs up - on _ my mind, _ Or _
with the town_ of Lim — er - ick have I an - y fault to find. _

Oh, the girl I love is beautiful,
She is fairer than the dawn.
She lives in Garryowen, my boys,
And is called the Cailín Bán.
She kept the enemy out all night,
Until the clear day dawned.
Most worthy of all my titles
Is this darling **Cailín Bán.**

Her skin is whiter than the snow
All on the mountain side;
And softer than the creamy foam
That flows down by the tide.
Her eyes are brighter than the dew
That sparkles on the lawn.
She is the sunshine of my heart,
My darling Cailín Bán.

Sung to the last 8 measures

Oh, the girl I love is beautiful
And fairer than the dawn.
She lives in Garryowen, my boys,
And is called the Cailín Bán.

*Cailín Bán – Maiden Fair

45

Finnegan's Wake

This British Victorian music-hall stereotyped vision of the Irish would have been just another relic of an insensitive era if it were not for the fact that James Joyce took the title for his famous book. That act elevated this song onto another plane for, as Irish folk singer and folklorist Patrick Galvin comments: "Joyce took the not-so-dead Finnegan as symbolic of Ireland herself, which gives the song a literary and historical interest which has nothing to do with the actual words. The use of such a song with this symbolic purpose was clearly satirical on Joyce's part." Dominic Behan, singer and poet, drops the possessive apostrophe and cries out: "Finnegans, wake!"

One mornin' Tim was rather full,
His head felt heavy which made him shake,
He fell from a ladder, and he broke his skull,
And they carried him home his corpse to wake.
They rolled him up in a nice clean sheet
And laid him out upon the bed,
With a gallon of whisky at his feet,
And a barrel of porter at his head. *Chorus*

His friends assembled at the wake,
And Mrs. Finnegan called for lunch,
First they brought in tay and cake,

Then pipes, tobacco and whisky punch.
Biddy O'Brien began to cry,
"Such a nice clean corpse did you ever see?
Tim Mavourneen why did you die?"
"Arrah hold your gob," said Paddy McGhee.
Chorus

Then Maggie O'Connor took up the job,
"Oh, Biddy," says she, "you're wrong I'm sure."
Biddy gave her a belt in the gob,
And left her sprawling on the floor.
Then the war did soon engage,

'Twas woman to woman, and man to man,
Shelelaigh law was all the rage,
And a row and a ruction soon began. *Chorus*

Then Mickey Maloney ducked his head,
When a noggin of whisky flew at him,
It missed and falling on the bed,
The liquor scattered over Tim.
Tim revives see how he rises,
Timothy rising from the bed
Said, "Whirl your whisky around like blazes,
Devil take my soul, do you think I'm dead?"
Chorus

46

The Old Turf Fire

"The life of the Gaels is so pitiable, so dark and sad and sorrowful, and they are so broken, bruised, and beaten – down in their own land and country that their talents and ingenuity find no place for themselves, and no way to let themselves out but in excessive foolish mirth, or in keening and lamentation." (Douglas Hyde, *Love Songs of Connacht,* 1893)

Oh, the old turf fire ____ and the hearth swept clean, There is no one half so hap-py as my-self and Pad-dy Keane. With the ba - by in the cra-dle you could hear her mam-my say, "Would-n't you go to sleep, a - lan - na, till I wet your dad-dy's tay."

Dm
Oh, the man that I work for is a richer man than me,
C
But somehow in this world, faith, we never can agree.
Dm   Am
He has big towering mansions and castles over all,
Dm
But sure I wouldn't exchange with him my little marble hall.

Dm
I have got a little house and a tidy bit of land.
C
You would never see a better one on the side of Knocknacran.
Dm   Am
I've no piano in the corner and no pictures on the wall,
Dm
But I'm somehow quite contented in my little marble hall.

Repeat first verse

The Bold Tenant Farmer

"Low prices in Ireland meant eviction, despair and, of course the reign of 'Captain Moonlight' with its usual accompaniments. Ricks were burned; cattle maimed; graves dug before doors and sometimes filled as well. Persons whose property or profession accustomed them to the receipt of threatening letters now found that they had a new correspondent, one 'Rory of the Hills, who always warns before he kills.' Among those who met his fate was Lord Mountmorris, despatched in his stronghold in County Galway." (*The Damnable Question: One Hundred and Twenty Years of Anglo-Irish Conflict* by George Dangerfield)

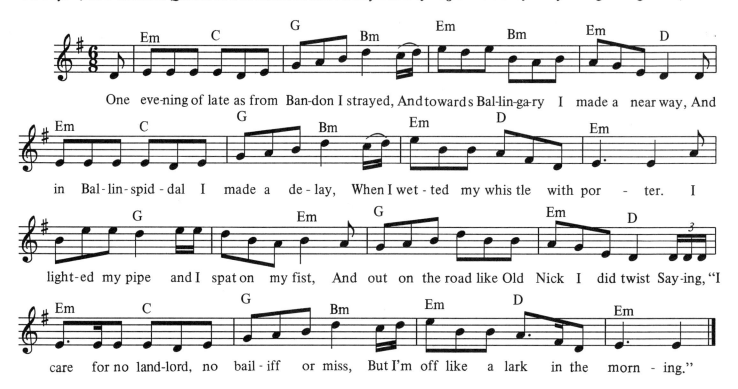

One eve-ning of late as from Ban-don I strayed, And towards Bal-lin-ga-ry I made a near way, And in Bal-lin-spid-dal I made a de-lay, When I wet-ted my whis-tle with por - ter. I light-ed my pipe and I spat on my fist, And out on the road like Old Nick I did twist Say-ing, "I care for no land-lord, no bail-iff or miss, But I'm off like a lark in the morn - ing."

    Em   C   G   Bm
I wasn't a scarce a mile out on the road,
    Em   Bm   Em   D
When I heard a great fight in a farmer's abode,
    Em   C   G   Bm
By the son of a landlord (an ill-looking toad),
    Em   D   Em
And the wife of a poor tenant farmer.
       G   Em
"Oh what in the divil comes over you all?
 G   Em   D
We can't get our rent when for it we do call,
   Em
But sure at next Sessions you'll pay for it all,
   Em   D   Em
Or you'll get the high road to Dungarven.

Sung to last 8 measures
    Em   G   Em
"Your husband was drinking in town t'other night,
 G   Em   D
And shouting and fighting for bold tenant's right,
    Em   C   G   Bm
But our plan of campaign will give him a fright."
    Em   D   Em
"Oh, we'll bear every wind in your storm.

       Em   C   G   Bm
"If my husband was drinking, now what's that to you?
     Em   Bm   Em   D
I'd rather he'd drink it than give it to you.
     Em   C   G   Bm
You hungry old miser, you're not worth a chew
     Em   D   Em
And your mossy old land is no bargain."
       G   Em
He shouted "hooray" and she shouted "hooroo",
 G   Em   D
And over the fields like Old Nick he flew,
     Em   C   G   Bm
Saying "May God help the landlords and old Ireland too!"
     Em   D   Em
Agus fag aimis siudh a ta se!*

Dungarven – the country jail   *literally: Let us leave that as it is.

Tigaree Torum Orum

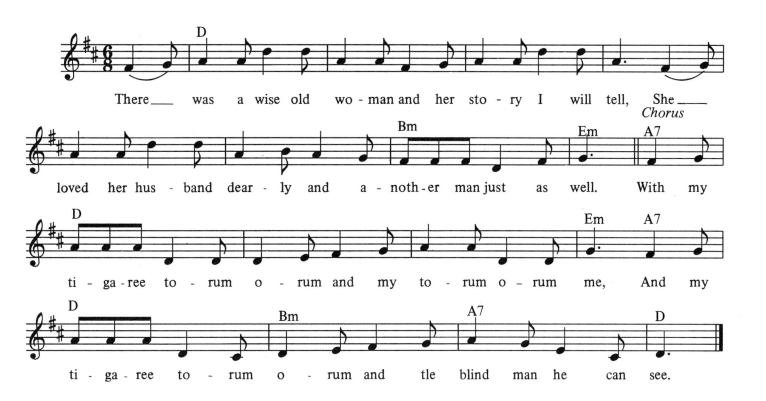

There was a wise old wo-man and her sto-ry I will tell, She
loved her hus-band dear-ly and a-noth-er man just as well. With my
ti-ga-ree to-rum o-rum and my to-rum o-rum me, And my
ti-ga-ree to-rum o-rum and tle blind man he can see.

D
Now, she went into the doctor's shop,

Some medecine for to buy.

She asked the doctor **kindly,**
Bm   Em
What would close the old man's eye. *Chorus*

D
"Now get for him some marrow **bones,**

And make him suck them all,

And when he has the last one sucked,
Bm   Em
He cannot see you at all." *Chorus*

D
Now the doctor sent for this old man,

And told him what she spoke.

He thanked the doctor kindly
Bm   Em
And he said he'd play the joke. *Chorus*

D
Now, she got for him the marrow bones,

And she made him suck them all,

And when he had the last one sucked,
Bm   Em
He couldn't see her at all. *Chorus*

D
"In this world I have no comfort,

And it's here I can't remain.

Sure I'll go out and drown myself,
Bm   Em
If I could see the stream." *Chorus*

D
"In this world you have no comfort,

And it's here you can't remain,

And if you like to drown yourself,
Bm   Em
I'll show you to the stream." *Chorus*

D
"Let me stand on the river bank,

And you run up the hill,

Then push me in with all your might."
Bm   Em
Says she, "My love, I will." *Chorus*

D
So he stood on the river bank

And she ran up the hill.

And when she ran down he slipped **aside,**
Bm   Em
And in the stream she fell. *Chorus*

D
She sank down to the **bottom,**

And she floated to the top.

He put a wattle to her side
Bm   Em
And he shoved her further off. *Chorus*

D
"Yirra, Johnny, dearest Johnny,

Are you leaving me behind?"

"Yirra, Nancy, dearest Nancy,
Bm   Em
Sure you thought you had me blind." *Chorus*

The Dingle Puck Goat

The highlight of the Puck Fair in Dingle is the crowning of the goat king. Puck (in Wales, Pwck) is the tree spirit who is believed to have the form of a goat. Like the Will o' the Wisp, he is a sprite who does no more harm than leading wanderers astray.

I am a young job-ber both fool-ish and air-y, The green hills of Ker-ry I came for to see. I went back to Din-gle to buy up some cat-tle, And I want you to lis-ten what hap-pened to me, As I en-tered the fair on a Sat-ur-day morn-ing, the first thing I saw was a long-leg-ged goat. Be-dad, and say, I for to com-mence our deal-ing, I think this bold he-ro is worth a pound note.

C
This daring old fellow I stood for to stare him,
    F   C   D7   G7
Although I feared he was a monster to see.
  C
He wore a long meggal as gray as a badger,
          F   C   G7 C
That would reach from Dingle to Cahirciveen.
     Em   Am   F   G7
With a pair of long horns like any two bayonets,
  Am   D7   G7
And just like two needles were pointed on top.
  C
I am very sure that you'd be a week laughing,
    F   C   G7   C
If only he happened to hit you a rap.

C
I made my approach to the owner that held him,
    F   C   D7   G7
A bargain we struck without much delay.
  C
He said if you pay me down twenty-two shillings,
         F   C   G7 C
Some advice I will give you before going away.
     Em   Am   F   G7
This daring young hero was reared on the mountains,
  Am   D7   G7
In the year sixty-four he first used to drill,
  C
And some of his comrades were hung and transported
    F   C   G7   C
And since he's determined some blood for to spill.

C
The old man departed and I was for starting.
        F   C   D7   G7
Those words that he told me put me in despair.
        C
The first jump he gave, well, he near broke my left arm.
     F   C   G7   C
I jumped on his back and got hold of his hair.
    Em   Am   F   G7
Says I, "My bold hero, on your back I'm landed,
       Am   D7   G7
And unless I will fall you may go where you will."
      C
He ran thro' the streets like something distracted,
       F   C   G7   C
And soon made his way towards Connor Hill.

           C
When he came near to Brandon I thought it was London;
     F   C   D7   G7
I regretted my journey when I saw the sea.
       C
He jumped into the water and swam right across it
    F   C   G7   C
Towards Castle Gregory over the way.
    Em   Am   F   G7
The waves of the ocean they put me in motion,
     Am   D7   G7
The fishes they ate all the nails off my toes,
       C
And a mighty big mackerel jumped for my nostrils,
      F   C   G7   C
And I thought he was gone with the half of my nose.

         C
When he came on the strand now quickly he ran
     F   C   D7   G7
Towards Clones or Castlemaine sure he did steer.
       C
To Milltown, Killorgin and likewise Killarney,
     F   C   G7   C
And never cried stop till he came to Kenmare.
    Em   Am   F   G7
At length then he spoke: "We have passed our headquarters.
    Am   D7   G7
It's where our ancestors always have been.
       C
Then let us return and take up our lodgings
     F   C   G7   C
At Curraghnamore where there's lots of poteen."

         C
We done our returns and stopped there till morning,
     F   C   D7   G7
It's during the night I sat up on his back.
       C
As the day it was dawning he jumped from the corner,
     F   C   G7   C
And t'wards Castleisland he went in a crack.
       Em   Am   F   G7
To the town of Tralee we next took our rambles.
    Am   D7   G7
I think he was anxious to see some more sport.
       C
Outside of the town we met some Highlanders
     F   C   G7   C
He up with his horns and he tore all their clothes.

         C
The Highlanders shouted and bawled, "Meela murder!
    F   C   D7   G7
Send for the polis and get him to jail."
        C
But the louder they shouted the faster my goat ran,
     F   C   G7   C
And over the Basin he gave them legbail.
      Em   Am   F   G7
On crossing the Basin I fell on the footway,
    Am   D7   G7
Away went the goat and I saw him no more.
      C
Sure if he's in Ireland he's in Camp or in Brandon,
     F   C   G7   C
Or away in the mountains somewhere remote. . . . *to Coda*

Coda

But while I am liv-ing I've a sto-ry worth tell-ing of my ram-bles thro' Ker-ry on the Din-gle puck goat.

Green Grows the Laurel

During the Mexican-American War of 1848, this song, with the title slightly altered to "Green Grow the Lilacs," was so popular among the American soldiers that speculation has it that it is the origin of the pejorative Mexican term for Americans: *gringo*. Another point that may be raised is — which "red, white and blue" is she referring to: the Stars and Stripes (emigration to America) or the Union Jack (perhaps joining the British army and sailing off to defend the Empire)?

I once had a sweet-heart, but it's now I have none, And since he has
left me I live all a - lone. I live all a - lone and con -
tent - ed I'll be, For he loves a - noth - er far bet - ter than me.

Chorus

Green grows the lau - rel and soft falls the dew, Sad was the
day when I part - ed from you. I hope our next meet-ing will
prove kind and true. Don't change the green lau - rel for the red, white and blue.

E
I wrote him a letter all crested in red;
B7
He wrote me an answer, and guess what he said.
E
"Keep your love letters and don't waste your time,
A   E   B7   E
Just write to your sweetheart and I'll write to mine." *Chorus*

E
I wonder and wonder why women love men,
B7
I wonder and never think how they love them.
E
For women are faithful and kind as you know,
A   E   B7   E
But men are deceivers wherever they go. *Chorus*

Garryowen

In 1868 the Seventh U.S. Cavalry under General George A. Custer was engaged in a campaign against the Cheyennes in Wyoming. On the morning of November 26, the regiment discovered the camp of Chief Black Kettle. At dawn, just as the bugles were sounding the charge, the band struck up "Garryowen." That day victory was Custer's. Eight years later, Custer heard his favorite tune for the last time when he marched out of Fort Lincoln headed for the Little Bighorn.

Let _ Bac - chus' sons _ be not _ dis - mayed, But _ join _ with me _ each jo - vi - al blade, Come _ booze _ and sing _ and lend _ your aid, To help _ me with _ the cho - rus. In - stead of spa we'll drink down ale, And _ pay the reck - 'ning on the nail, No man for debt shall go to jail From Gar - ry - o - wen in glo - ry.

C   Am
We are the boys that take delight in
C   G
Smashing the Limerick lights when lighting.
C   Em
Through all the streets like sporters fighting,
C   G
And tearing all before us. *Chorus*

C   Am
We'll beat the bailiffs out of fun,
C   G
We'll make the mayors and sheriffs run;
C   Em
We are the boys no man dares dun,
C   G
If he regards a whole skin. *Chorus*

C   Am
We'll break the windows, we'll break the doors,
C   G
The watch knock down by threes and fours;
C   Em
Then let the doctors work their cures,
C   G
And tinker up our bruises. *Chorus*

C   Am
Our hearts so stout have got us fame,
C   G
For soon 'tis known from whence we came;
C   Em
Where'er we go they dread the name
C   G
Of Garryowen in glory. *Chorus*

The Hounds of Filemore

Thade Bowler was a 19th-century schoolmaster and sportsman. He was a tenant on the Carhan estate of Daniel O'Connell (1775–1847), the Irish statesman and Member of the British Parliament. As a boy, Bowler frequently took part in what were called "drag hunts" with O'Connell himself.

You lads and lass-es gay, And you with sport-ing fa-ces, If you live un-to next year, You will ne'er for-get the ra-ces. Such ra-ces we will have, With out bri-dle, whip or sad-dle, And none of you will say That it's all a fid-dle fad-dle. *Chorus* Oh,— File-more you're the place for— mer-ry sport and sing-ing, And the chief a-mong them all is the charm-ing bea-gle hunt-ing.

G D7 A drag hunt we will have, G D G Swift horses and fine riders. D7 Gentlemen there will be, G For to wield their swords and sabres. D7 If a single man should fall, G D G We will all feel very sorry, D7 For a sign it is most sure. G That year he will not marry. *Chorus*	G D7 Comely struck it first. G D G There was Rattler Thade the Weaver. D7 Small Truman from Tureen, G And Tanner was their leader. D7 Juno Coffey of Coars, G D G Likewise Juno of Foley. D7 Juno Lynch indeed, G Were three Junos full of glory. *Chorus*
G D7 Around the course we'll go, G D G To see who'll rouse the echo D7 From Carhan woods above, G To the mountains of Kimego. D7 Kenmare will hear the shock, G D G And Dingle will awaken. D7 Killorglin will resound, G And Valentia will be shaken. *Chorus*	G D7 And now the hunt is over, G D G The sun is nearly setting. D7 Into town we'll go, G As tired our limbs are getting. D7 In tap rooms we will sit, G D G Call for porter, ale and whisky. D7 Then homeward we will go, G With spirits light and frisky. *Chorus*

The Cork Leg

The "comic Dutchman" was a stock character in the British music hall. "Villikens and His Dinah" (whose melody we know as "Sweet Betsy from Pike") is another good example of the genre. This version of "The Cork Leg" comes from County Tyrone.

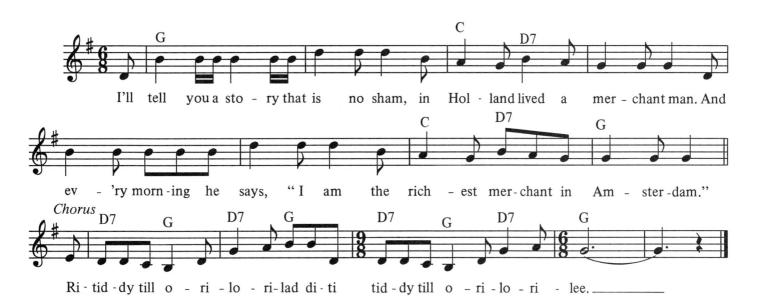

I'll tell you a story that is no sham, in Holland lived a merchant man. And ev'ry morning he says, "I am the richest merchant in Amsterdam."

Chorus

Ri - tid - dy till o - ri - lo - ri - lad di - ti tid - dy till o - ri - lo - ri - lee._____

G
One day he sat as full as an egg,
  C   D7   G
When a poor relation came to beg,

He kicked him out with a brogue and a keg,
  C   D7   G
And kicking him out, he broke a leg. *Chorus*

G
He told his friends he had got hurt,
C   D7   G
"By a friend I have lost a foot,

And upon crutches I never will walk,
     C   D7   G
For I'll have a beautiful leg of cork." *Chorus*

G
A doctor came on his vocation,
  C D7   G
And over it made a long oration,

And just to save his reputation,
  C   D7   G
He finished it off with an amputation. *Chorus*

G
When the leg was on and finished right,
     C   D7   G
When the leg was on they screwed it tight.

But still he went with a bit of a hop,
       C   D7   G
When he found the leg it would't stop. *Chorus*

G
O'er hedges and ditches and scaur and plain,
       C   D7   G
To rest his weary limbs he'd fain.

He threw himself down, but all in vain,
     C   D7   G
The leg got up and away. again. *Chorus*

G
He called to them that were in sight,
     C   D7   G
"Stop me or I'm wounded quite."

Although their aid he did invite,
     C   D7   G
In less than a minute he was out of sight. *Chorus*

G
And he kept running from place to place,
      C   D7   G
The people thought he was running a race,

He clung to a post for to stop the pace,
       C   D7   G
But the leg it still kept up the chase. *Chorus*

G
Over hedges and ditches and plain and scaur,
      C   D7   G
And Europe he has travelled o'er.

Although he's dead and is no more,
      C   D7   G
The leg goes on as it did before. *Chorus*

G
So often you see in broad daylight
  C   D7   G
A skeleton on a cork leg tight.

Although the artist did him invite,
     C   D7   G
He never was **paid,** and it served him right. *Chorus*

The County of Mayo

Words by Thomas La Nelle

Tune: "Billy Byrne of Ballymanus"

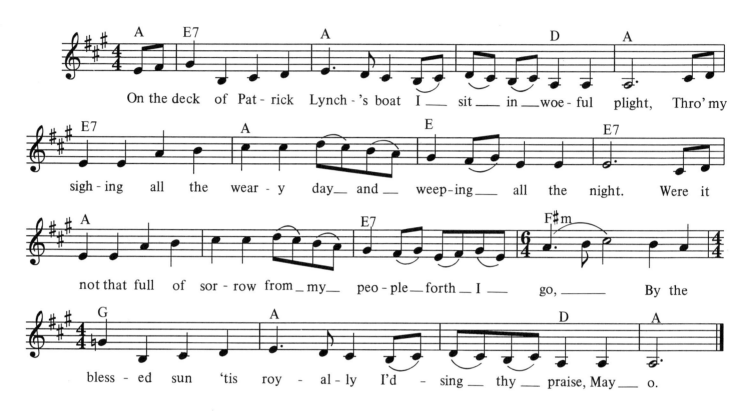

On the deck of Pat-rick Lynch-'s boat I __ sit __ in __ woe-ful plight, Thro' my sigh-ing all the wear-y day __ and __ weep-ing __ all the night. Were it not that full of sor-row from __ my __ peo-ple __ forth __ I __ go, __ By the bless-ed sun 'tis roy-al-ly I'd-sing __ thy __ praise, May __ o.

<pre>
A   E7   A   D   A
When I dwelt at home in plenty and my gold did much abound,
          E7   A   E   E7
In the company of fair young maids the Spanish ale went 'round.
     A   E7   F♯m
'Tis a bitter change from those gay days that now I'm forced to go,
          G   A   D   A
And must leave my bones in Santa Cruz, far from my own Mayo.
</pre>

<pre>
A   E7   A   D   A
They are altered girls in Irrul now - 'tis proud they're grown and high,
          E7   A   E   E7
With their hair-bags and their topknots, for I pass their buckles by.
     A   E7   F♯m
But 'tis little little now I heed their airs for God will have it so,
          G   A   D   A
That I must depart for foreign lands, and leave my sweet Mayo.
</pre>

<pre>
A   E7   A   D   A
"Tis my grief that Patrick Loughlin is not Earl in Irrul still,
          E7   A   E   E7
And that Bryan Duff no longer rules as lord upon the hill,
          A   E7   F♯m
And that Colonel Hugh O'Grady should be lying dead and low,
          G   A   D   A
And I sailing, sailing swiftly from the County of Mayo.
</pre>

McCaffery

John McCaffery was found guilty of murdering an officer, and executed in Liverpool in 1882.

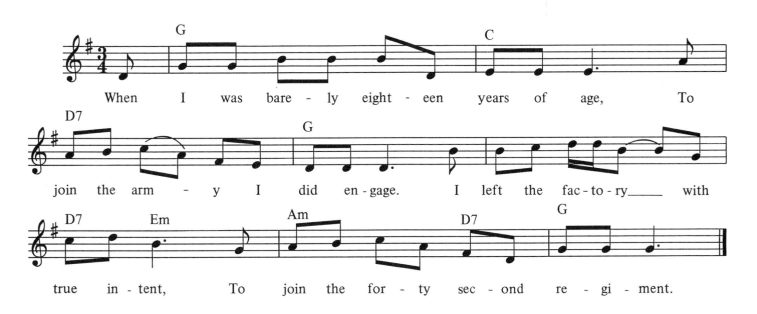

To Fulwood Barracks I then did go,
To spend some time in that depot.
But fortunate I was not to be,
For Captain Hansom took a dislike to me.

It happened that I was on guard one day,
Three sergeants' children came out to play.
I took one's name instead of all three,
With neglect of duty they did charge me.

At Fulwood guardroom I did appear,
But Captain Hansom my case would not hear,
So to my fate I was resigned
And in Fulwood guardroom I was confined.

For thirteen weeks my hatred grew.
It filled my body all through and through,
Until the deed I resolved one night,
Was to shoot Captain Hansom dead on sight.

Early one morning on the barrack square
Captain Hansom was walking with Colonel Blair,
I raised my rifle; I shot to kill.
But I shot my colonel against my will.

I done the deed, I shed the blood.
At Liverpool Assizes my trial I stood.
Judge says to me, "McCaffery,
Prepare yourself for the gallows tree."

I had no father to take my part,
Likewise no mother to break her heart.
Only one pal and a girl was she —
She'd have laid down her life for McCaffery.

Come all you young Irishmen, come listen to me,
Have nothing to do with the British Army.
For only lies and tyranny
Made a murderer out of McCaffery.

Felix the Soldier

The Seven Years' War (1756–1763), which pitted coalitions of European powers against each other, spilled over into America as a conflict between England and France. The Indian nations allied themselves with France in what was, essentially, a colonial war. They did not realize it, but they stood to lose no matter who won the French and Indian War, as it came to be known on this side of the Atlantic. Although Britain's victory consolidated its position in North America, the vast expenditures of the war forced it to impose new taxation ("without representation") on the Colonies: the Sugar Act and the Stamp Act. This had the effect of leading to the serious beginnings of the movement for American independence. The French and Indian War not only gave the young George Washington his first taste of battle, but also introduced many an Irish conscript to the joys and sorrows of "North Americay."

They took a-way my brogues And they robbed me of my spade; They
put me in the ar - my And a sol - dier of me made.

E
But I couldn't beat the drum,
B7
And I couldn't play the flute,

So they handed me a musket
E   B7   E
And taught me how to shoot.

E
We had bloody fight
B7
After we had scaled the wall,

And the divil a bit of mercy
E   B7   E
Did the Frenchies have at all.

E
But the Injuns they were sly,
B7
And the Frenchies they were coy,

So they shot off the left leg
E   B7   E
Of this poor Irish boy.

E
Then they put me on a ship
B7
And they sent me home again,

With all my army training
E   B7   E
After battle's strife and din.

E
I will bid my spade adieu,
B7
For I cannot dig the bog,

But still can play a fiddle
E   B7   E
And I still can drink my grog.

E
I have learned to smoke a pipe,
B7
And have learned to fire a gun.

To the divil with the fighting,
E   B7   E
I am glad the war is done.

The Sons of Liberty

Irish conscripts in the British army took a dim view of fighting the king's wars under any circumstances - all the more so when it involved battling the "sons of liberty."

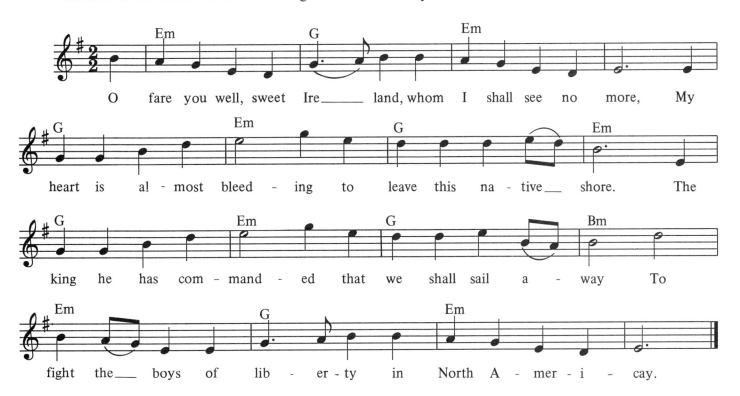

O fare you well, sweet Ire____ land, whom I shall see no more, My heart is al - most bleed – ing to leave this na - tive____ shore. The king he has com - mand - ed that we shall sail a - way To fight the____ boys of lib - er - ty in North A - mer - i - cay.

Em G Em
It was early in the morning, just at the break of day,
G Em G Bm
We hoisted British colors and anchored in Yorks Bay.
G Em G Bm
The sails a-being lassered they spread abroad to dry,
Em G Em
The Irish heroes landing, but the Lord knows who must die.

Em G Em
Through fields of blood we waded where the cannons loudly roar,
G Em G Em
And many a galliant soldier lay a-bleeding in his gore,
G Em G Bm
And it's many a gallant commander, it's on the field did lay,
Em G Em
That was both killed and wounded by the Sons of Liberty.

Em G Em
Your hearts would have melted with pity to have seen the soldiers' wives,
G Em G Em
A-hunting for their dead husbands and the melancholy cries,
G Bm G Bm
And the children crying, "Mother, we surely rue the day
Em G Em
When we came for to lose our father dear in the North Americay."

Em G Em
Here's an end to my ditty, my song is at an end,
G Em G Em
Here's health to General Washington and all of his bold men,
G Em G Bm
God help a man protect him that is by land or sea,
Em G Em
For he had boys who feared no noise - the Sons of Liberty.

The Irishman's Epistle

Listen my children, and you shall hear
Of the midnight ride of Paul Revere,
On the eighteenth of April, in Seventy-five;
Hardly a man is now alive
Who remembers that famous day and year. . . .

You know the rest, in the books you have read,
How the British Regulars fired and fled,
How the farmers gave them ball for ball,
From behind each fence and farmyard wall. . . .
(From "Paul Revere's Ride" by Henry Wadsworth Longfellow)

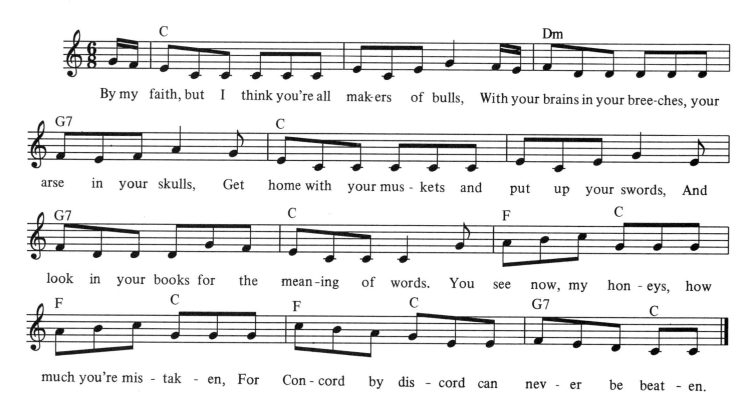

By my faith, but I think you're all mak-ers of bulls, With your brains in your bree-ches, your arse in your skulls, Get home with your mus-kets and put up your swords, And look in your books for the mean-ing of words. You see now, my hon-eys, how much you're mis-tak-en, For Con-cord by dis-cord can nev-er be beat-en.

     C
How brave ye went out with your muskets all bright,
  Dm   G7
And thought to befrighten the folks with the sight;
  C
But when you got there how they powdered your pums,
  G7   C
And all the way home how they peppered your bums;
  F   C   F   C
And is it not, honeys, a comical crack,
    F   C   G7   C
To be proud in the face and be shot in the back.

     C
With all of your talkin' and all of your wordin',
  Dm   G7
And all of your shoutin' and marchin' and swordin',
       C
How come ye to think now they didn't know how
  G7   C
To be after their firelocks as smartly as you?
    F   C   F   C
You see now, my honeys, 'tis nothing at all,
    F   C   G7   C
But to pull at the trigger and pop goes the ball.

     C
And what have you got now with all your designing,
    Dm   G7
But a town without victuals to sit down and dine in;
    C
And to look on the ground like a parcel of noodles,
   G7   C
And sing, how the Yankees have beaten the Doodles.
     F   C   F   C
I'm sure if you're wise you'll make peace for a dinner,
     F   C   G7   C
For fighting and fasting will soon make you thinner.

Whisky, You're the Devil

The "march" is the frontier, the border. When you "ran for march," you were on your way. Between 1846 and 1891 more than three million Irish immigrants arrived in America.

O now, brave boys we'll run for march, And not to Por-tu-gal or Spain, The drums are beat-ing, ban-ners flying, The dev-il at home we'll find to-night. O,

Chorus
love, fare thee well, with me ti-ther-ee - i doo-dle-um-a-day, with me ti-ther-ee - i doo-dle-um-a-day, My right-fol toor-a-lad-die o, there's whis-ky in the jar. Whis-ky, you're the dev-il, you're lead-ing me a-stray, O-ver hills and moun-tains and to A-mer-i-cay, You're strong-er, sweet-er, de-cent-er, you're spunk-i-er than tay, O, ___ whis-ky, you're my dar-ling, drunk or so-ber.

D
Oh the French are fighting boldly,

Em   A7
Men are dying hot and cowardly,

Bm   D
Give every man his flask of powder,

E7   A7
His firelock on his shoulder.   *Chorus*

D
Says the mother, "Do not wrong me,

Em   A7
Don't take my daughter from me,

Bm   D
For if you do I shall torment you,

E7   A7
And after that me ghost will haunt you."   *Chorus*

Across the Western Ocean

In this typical sea chantey, the leader, or chantyman, sings the first and third lines and the crew, the second and fourth. Amelia could have been a girl's name or, perhaps, the name of a ship: the *Amelia Strong*. The Irish army (in verse two) refers to the mass of people leaving starving Ireland.

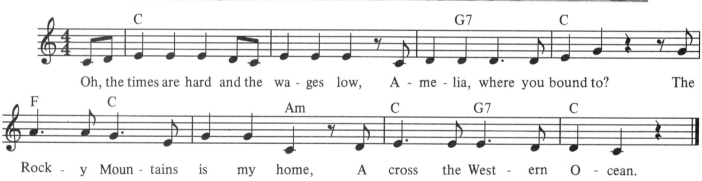

Oh, the times are hard and the wa-ges low, A-me-lia, where you bound to? The Rock-y Moun-tains is my home, A cross the West-ern O-cean.

C
The land of promise there you'll see,
G7   C
Amelia, where you bound to?
    F   C   Am
I'm bound across that Western sea,
    C   G7 C
To join the Irish army.

C
To Liverpool I'll take my way,
G7   C
Amelia, where you bound to?
    F   C   Am
To Liverpool that Yankee school,
    C   G7   C
Across the Western Ocean.

C
There's Liverpool Pat with his tarpaulin hat,
G7   C
Amelia, where you bound to?
      F   C   Am
And Yankee John, the packet rat.
    C   G7   C
Across the Western Ocean.

C
Beware the packet ships, I say.
G7   C
Amelia, where you bound to?
    F   C   Am
They steal your stores and clothes away,
    C   G7   C
Across the Western Ocean.

No Irish Wanted Here

When the poor Irish immigrants arrived in America they faced an often less than enthusiastic reception. The next two songs address the same problem from somewhat different perspectives: the first, "serious and noble"; the second, "comic and violent." The British folklorist A. L. Lloyd had this to say, re "No Irish Need Apply": "Some say it's a mockery of the Irish; others say it's a good historical protest song. The nub of the matter seems to be that the song exists in many versions, some more stage Irish than others, but all of them positive satires on an ugly piece of race discrimination. To me there seems to be no doubt that the song was originally made by Irishmen, and that many of the more stagey versions are the work of sincere Irishmen too. I've never seen a version that was so mock Irish that the song lost its bite. But for those hypersensitive souls who find the more familiar texts offensive, here is a Nova Scotia version which is less humorous and more earnest than most."

Chorus:

    G   C   D7 G
You may think it a misfortune to be christened Pat or Dan.
    C   G   A7   D
To me it is an honor to be called an Irishman,
    C   G   A7   D
And you may live to see the day, it will come, oh never fear,
    Em   G   A7   D7 G
When ignorance gives way to sense: You're welcome, Irish, here.

    G   C   D7 G
When your country was in danger but a few short years ago.
    C   G   A7   D
You were not so particular about who should fight the foe,
    C   G   A7   D
When men were needed for the ranks to preserve our rights so dear,
    Em   G   A7   D7 G
Among the bravest of the brave, it was: "Irish wanted here".   *Chorus*

    G   C   D7   G
For generous hearts and charity you could search this wide world 'round,
    C   G   A7   D
For Paddy's hospitality its like was never found,
    C   G   A7   D
He'd give the clothes from off his back, his blood for friends so dear,
    Em   G   A7   D7 G
But through injustice and vile envy there's no Irish wanted here. *Chorus*

    G   C   D7   G
Then turn your hearts to kindness, take poor Paddy from the wall,
    C   G   A7   D
For God in heaven made this world with lots of room for all,
    C   G   A7   D
So stretch your arms scross the sea to that little isle so dear,
    Em   G   A7   D7 G
And give the Irish girls and boys glad welcome over here. *Chorus*

63

No Irish Need Apply

I'm a de-cent boy just land-ed from the town of Bal-ly
seen em-ploy-ment ad-ver-tised, 'tis just the thing says

fad,___ I want a sit-u-a-tion and I want it ver-y
I, But the dirt-y spal-peen end-ed with, "No

bad. I have I-rish need ap-ply. "Whoo!" says I, "but that's an

in-sult, tho' to get the place I'll try,"___ So I went to see this

black-guard with his "No I-rish need ap-ply." Some do

count it a mis-for-tune to be chris-tened Pat or Dan, But to

me it is an hon-or to be born an I-rish man.___

C
I started out to find the house,
F   G7
I got it mighty soon,
C   F
There I found the old chap seated,
C   G7
He was reading the Tribune.
C
I told him what I came for,
F   G7
When he in a rage did fly,
C   F
"No," he says, "You are a Paddy,
C   G7   C
And no Irish need apply."
F
Then I gets my dander rising,
C
And I'd like to black his eye,
D7
To tell an Irish gentleman,
G   D7   G
"No Irish need apply." *Chorus*

C
I couldn't stand it longer
F   G7
So ahold of him I took,
C   F
And gave him such a welting
C   G7
As he'd get at Donnybrook.
C
He hollered, "Millia Murther,"
F   G7
And to get away did try,
C   F
And swore he'd never write again,
C   G7   C
"No Irish need apply."
F
Well, he made a big apology,
C
I bid him then good-bye,
D7
Saying, "When next you want a beating,
G   D7   G
Write "No Irish need apply." *Chorus*

64

Drill, Ye Tarriers, Drill

"This is a good country for a labouring man. At this time he can earn at least one dollar a day, equal to 4 shillings British. He is in good demand for this sum. He can board himself well—having meat three times a day, for ten dollars a month. . . . Believe me, there is no idle bread to be had here. If you get a dollar a day, you have to earn it well." (From an 1853 letter of a young Irish immigrant)

Ev - 'ry morn ing at sev - en o' clock, There were twen - ty tar - ri - ers a - work-ing at the rock, And the boss comes a - round and he says, "Keep still, And come down heav-y on the cast iron drill," And drill, ye tar - ri - ers, drill. Drill, ye tar - ri - ers, drill For it's work all day for the su - gar in your tay, Down be - hind the rail - way, And drill, ye tar - ri - ers, drill, and blast, and fire

Am
Now, our new foreman was Jim McCann,
E7
By God, he was a blame mean man,
Am
Last week a premature blast went off,
E7
And a mile in the air went Big Jim Goff, *Chorus*

Am
The next time payday come around,
E7
Jim Goff a dollar short was found.
Am
When he asked, "What for?" came this reply,
E7
"You're docked for the time you was up in the sky." *Chorus*

Am
Now, the boss was a fine man down to the ground,
E7
And he married a lady six feet round;
Am
She baked good bread and she baked it well,
E7
But she baked it hard as the holes in hell, *Chorus*

65

Fillimiooriay

In eight-een hun-dred and for-ty -one, I put my cor-du-roy breech-es on, I put my cor-du-roy breech-es on, To work up-on the rail - way.

Chorus

Fill - i - mi - oo - ri - oo - ri - ay, Fil - i - mi - oo - ri - oo - ri - ay,

Fil - i - mi - oo - ri - oo - ri - ay, To work up - on the rail - way.

Am
In eighteen hundred and forty-two,
C
I left the old world for the new,
Am
Bad cess to the luck that brought me through.
G   Am
To work upon the railway. *Chorus*

Am
In eighteen hundred and forty-three,
C
'Twas then I met sweet Biddy McGee,
Am
An elegant wife she's been to me,
G   Am
While working on the railway. *Chorus*

Am
In eighteen hundred and forty-four,
C
I worked again, and worked some more,
Am
It's "Bend your backs," the boss did roar,
G   Am
While working on the railway. *Chorus*

Am
It's "Pat, do this," and "Pat, do that,"
C
Without a stocking or cravat,
Am
And nothing but an old straw hat,
G   Am
While working on the railway. *Chorus*

Am
In eighteen hundred and forty-five,
C
They worked us worse than bees in a hive,
Am
I didn't know if I was dead or alive,
G   Am
While working on the railway. *Chorus*

Am
In eighteen hundred and forty-six,
C
They pelted me with stones and sticks,
Am
Oh, I was in a terrible fix,
G   Am
While working on the railway. *Chorus*

Am
In eighteen hundred and forty-seven,
C
Sweet Biddy McGee, she went to heaven.
Am
If she left one child, she left eleven,
G   Am
To work upon the railway. *Chorus*

The Bowld Soger Boy

This dates back to the early 1850s. During the Civil War it was popular with Northern and Southern regiments alike.

By Samuel Lover

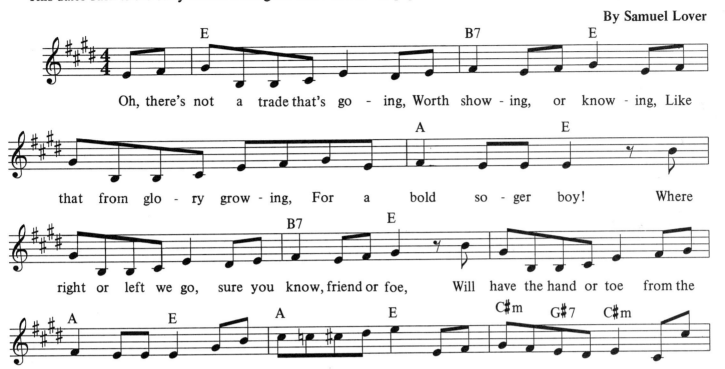

Oh, there's not a trade that's go - ing, Worth show - ing, or know - ing, Like

that from glo - ry grow - ing, For a bold so - ger boy! Where

right or left we go, sure you know, friend or foe, Will have the hand or toe from the

bowld so - ger boy. There's not a town we march through, But the la - dies look - ing arch though the

win - dow panes will sarch through the ranks to find their joy. While up the street each girl you meet, with

look so sly will cry, "My eye! oh, is - n't he the dar - ling, The bowld so - ger boy!"

E
But when we get the route,
 B7   E
How they pout, and they shout,

While to the right about
 A   E
Goes the bowld soger boy!

'Tis then that lassies fair,
 B7   E
In despair tear their hair.

 A   B7   C#m   B7
We taste her tap, we tear her cap;
 E   B7   E
"Oh, that's the chap for me,"
 A   B7   E
Says she. "Oh, isn't he a darling,
 A   Am   E
The bowld soger boy."

But, "The Divil a one I care,"
 A   E
Says the bowld soger boy.
 A   E
For the world is all before us
 C#m G#7   C#m
Where the landladies adore us
 A   E
And never refuse to score us,
 C#m G#7   C#m
But chalk us up with joy.

Since I've Been in the Army

This song appeared in a book of popular songs shortly before the Civil War. Despite its "Irish lyrics" the tune is an old Scottish one: "Wha'll Be King But Charlie?"

Em   G
The lots of girls my train unfurls would make a dacent party,
D7   G   D   G   Em
There's Katy Lynch, a tidy wench, and Peg and Sue McCarty;

                                                      G
There's Sally Maggs, and Judy Braggs, and Martha Scraggs, all storm me;
     D7 G   D   G   Em
And Molly Magee, she's after me, since I've been in the army.
                                                        B7   Em
The Kittys and the Dollys, the Bridgets and the Pollys, in numbers would alarm ye;
          G   Em
Even Mrs. White, that's lost her sight, admires me in the army.   *Chorus*

      Em
The roaring boys, they made a noise, and whacked me like the divil,
D7 G   D   G   Em
And now become before me dumb, or else they're mighty civil.

                                                      G
There's Murphy Rourke, that often broke my head, now daresn't dare me,
D7 G   D   G   Em
But bows and scrapes, and off he sneaks, since I've been in the army.

                                                 B7   Em
An' if one neglect to pay me respect, another tips the blarney,
    G   Em
Wid, "Whist, my friend, an' don't offend a gintleman in the army.'"

    Em   G
My arms are bright, my heart is light, good humor seems to warm me,
D7 G   D   G   Em
I'm now become, wid every chum, a favorite in the army.

                                                  G
If I go on as I've begun, my comrades all inform me,
    D7 G   D   G   Em
They plainly see that I shall be a Gineral in the army.
                                                B7   Em
Delightful, notion, to get promotion! Ye ladies thin I'll charm ye;
     G   Em
For it's my belief, commander-in-chief, I soon shall be in the army;

68

The Seven Irishmen

The army recruiter is a recurrent and much-despised figure in Anglo-Irish-Scottish song. During the Crimean War, the recruiting sergeants would offer a likely young prospect a drink and then slip a shilling into the glass. The minute he put the glass to his lips he was politely, but ever so firmly, informed that he had just enlisted in the army, having taken the "king's shilling."

All — you that love the — sham rock green, at - tend, — both young and old. I feel it is — my du - ty those — lines for — you to un - fold, con - cern - ing those young em - i - grants who — late - ly — sailed — a way To seek a bet - ter live - li - hood all in A - mer - i - cay.

C
On the fourteenth day of April our noble ship did sail
          F C
        G   C   G
With fifty-five young Irishmen, true Sons of Grannuaille.
   C   G   C   G
They landed safely in New York on the nineteenth day of May,
C   Am   C F C
To see their friends and relatives all in Americay.

C
Some of them had friends to meet as soon as they did land.
             F C
        G C   G
With flowing bumpers drank a health to Poor old Paddy's land.
C   G   C   G
Those who had no friends to meet, their hearts were stout and bold,
C   Am   C F C
And by the cursed Yankees they would not be controlled.

C
Seven of those young Irishmen were walking through George's Street,
                F   C
     G C   G
When a Yankee officer they happened for to meet.
  C   G   C   G
He promised them employment in a brick yard near the town.
C   Am   C   F C
There he did conduct them; their names were taken down.

  C
He took them to an alehouse; he called for drinks galore.
              F C
  C   G C   G
I'm sure such entertainment they never had before.
C   G   C   G
When he thought he had them drunk, those words to them did say,
  C   Am   C F C
"You are 'listed now as soldier to defend Americay."

C
They looked at one another, those words they then did say,
              F C
        C G   C   G
"It's not to 'list that we did come into Americay,
   C   G C   G
But to labour for our livelihood as we often did before,
      C   Am C F C
And we lately emigrated from the lovely Shamrock shore."

         C
Twelve Yankees dressed as soldiers came in without delay.
        C G   C   G
They said, "My lads, you must prepare with us to come away.
         C G C   G
You signed with one of our officers, so you cannot now refuse,
C   Am   C   F   C
So prepare, my lads, to join our ranks, for you must pay your dues."

C
The Irish blood began to rise, one of those heroes said,
              F C
        C G C
"We have one only life to lose, therefore we're not afraid.
        C   G C   G
Although we are from Ireland, this day we'll let you see,
  C   Am   C F C
We'll die like Sons of Grannuaille and keep our liberty."

C
The Irish boys got to their feet, it made the Yankees frown.
              F   C
        G C   G
As fast as they could strike a blow, they knocked the soldiers down.
C   G   C   G
With bloody heads and broken bones, they left them in crimson gore,
C   Am   C F C
And proved themselves St. Patrick's Day, throughout Columbus' shore.

Morrissey and the Russian Sailor

John Morrissey was losing the fight to the challenger, James Ambrose ("Yankee Sullivan") in Boston on October 12, 1853, when Sullivan left the ring between rounds to slug a few heckling Morrissey fans. When he failed to get back into the ring by the bell, the decision was awarded to Morrissey. With his heavyweight title intact, Morrissey went on to defeat John Heenan, the "Benicia Boy." No record of this epic fight against the Russian sailor can be found, but the epic ballad stands. Morrissey, "the Irish boy who fought his way to fame and fortune," was born in Templemore, Ireland, in 1831. His family emigrated to Canada around 1835 and shortly thereafter moved south of the border. He amassed considerable wealth as heavyweight champion and, after retiring from the ring, built the Saratoga (New York) racetrack in 1864. He served as a Democratic Congressman from New York, 1867–1871. He died in 1878.

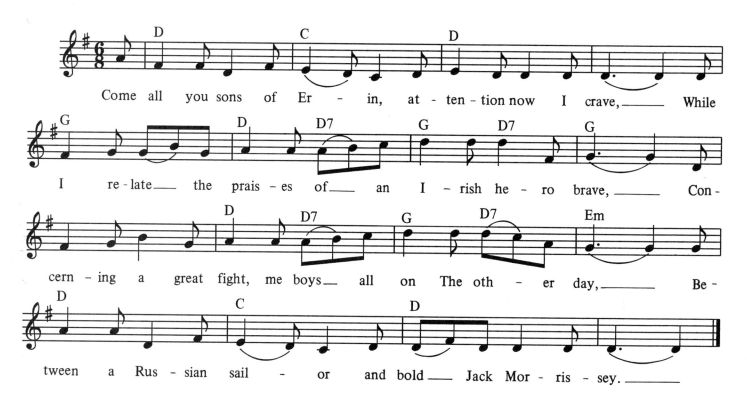

Come all you sons of Er - in, at - ten - tion now I crave, ____ While
I re - late ____ the prais - es of ____ an I - rish he - ro brave, ____ Con -
cern - ing a great fight, me boys ____ all on The oth - er day, ____ Be -
tween a Rus - sian sail - or and bold ____ Jack Mor - ris - sey. ____

     D   C   D
It was in Terra del Fuego, in South Americay,
    G   D   D7 G D7   G
The Russian challenged Morrissey and unto him did say,
             D   D7   G   D7 Em
"I hear you are a fighting man, and wear a belt I see.
     D   C   D
What do you say, will you consent to have a round with me?"

     D   C   D
Then up spoke bold Jack Morrissey, with a heart so stout and true,
    G   D D7 G D7   G
Saying, "I am a gallant Irishman that never was subdued.
         D D7 G D7   Em
Oh, I can whale a Yankee, a Saxon bull or bear,
   D   C   D
And in honor of old Paddy's land I'll still those laurels wear.

     D   C   D
These words enraged the Russian upon that foreign land,
    G   D D7   G D7 G
To think that he would be put down by any Irishman.
              D   D7   G   D7   Em
He says, "You are too light for me. On that make no mistake."
     D   C   D
I would have you to resign the belt, or else your life I'll take."

     D   C   D
To fight upon the tenth of June these heroes did agree,
    G   D D7   G D7 G
And thousands came from every part the battle for to see.
                D   D7 G   D7
The English and the Russians, their hearts were filled with
  Em
glee;
     D   C   D
They swore the Russian sailor boy would kill bold Morrissey.

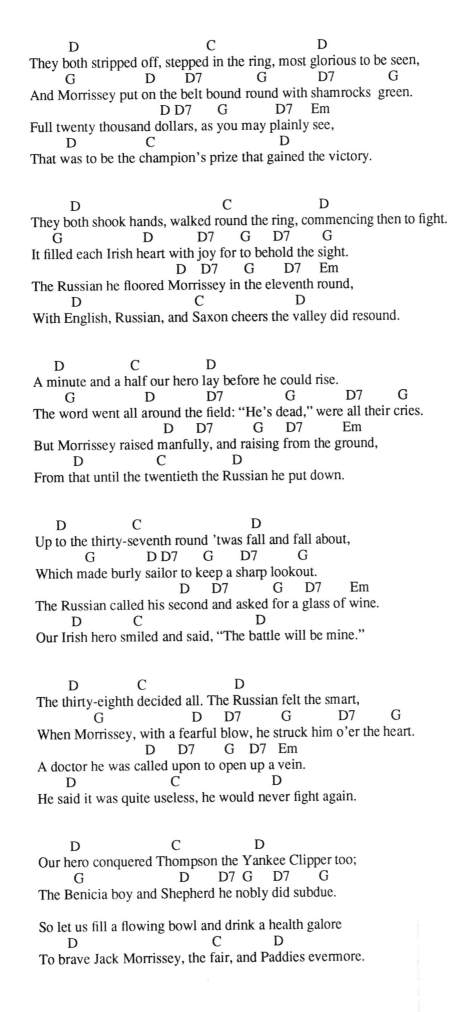

```
         D                      C                   D
They both stripped off, stepped in the ring, most glorious to be seen,
   G        D      D7        G        D7        G
And Morrissey put on the belt bound round with shamrocks  green.
                           D D7    G      D7   Em
Full twenty thousand dollars, as you may plainly see,
     D            C                 D
That was to be the champion's prize that gained the victory.


         D                      C               D
They both shook hands, walked round the ring, commencing then to fight.
   G        D       D7    G  D7    G
It filled each Irish heart with joy for to behold the sight.
                         D  D7    G     D7   Em
The Russian he floored Morrissey in the eleventh round,
     D              C                 D
With English, Russian, and Saxon cheers the valley did resound.


      D         C          D
A minute and a half our hero lay before he could rise.
   G          D        D7          G        D7      G
The word went all around the field: "He's dead," were all their cries.
                         D    D7    G    D7     Em
But Morrissey raised manfully, and raising from the ground,
     D            C          D
From that until the twentieth the Russian he put down.


      D          C              D
Up to the thirty-seventh round 'twas fall and fall about,
      G        D D7    G    D7       G
Which made burly sailor to keep a sharp lookout.
                         D     D7      G   D7    Em
The Russian called his second and asked for a glass of wine.
     D          C                D
Our Irish hero smiled and said, "The battle will be mine."


        D          C          D
The thirty-eighth decided all. The Russian felt the smart,
        G           D    D7     G      D7      G
When Morrissey, with a fearful blow, he struck him o'er the heart.
                        D   D7    G  D7  Em
A doctor he was called upon to open up a vein.
     D                C            D
He said it was quite useless, he would never fight again.


        D            C           D
Our hero conquered Thompson the Yankee Clipper too;
   G              D      D7  G   D7     G
The Benicia boy and Shepherd he nobly did subdue.


So let us fill a flowing bowl and drink a health galore
     D                    C        D
To brave Jack Morrissey, the fair, and Paddies evermore.
```

Michael Roy of Brooklyn City

This song first appeared in print in an 1856 songster. In 1888 it was included in a leaflet of songs to be sung at a Harvard Club dinner at Delmonico's Restaurant in New York.

In Brook-lyn Ci-ty there lived a maid And she was known to fame,____ Her moth-er's name was Ma-ry Ann and her's was Ma-ry Jane,____ And ev-'ry Sat-ur-day morn-ing she used to go o-ver the riv-er To Ful-ton Mar-ket where she sold eggs and sau-sag-es, like-wise liv-er.____ For Oh,____ for Oh,____ He was my dar-ling boy,____ For he was the lad with the au-burn hair and his name was Mi-chael Roy.____

C
She fell in love with a charcoal man,
G7   C
McCloskey was his name.

His fighting weight was seven stone ten,
     F   C
And he loved sweet Mary Jane.

He took her to ride in his charcoal cart
     F   C
On a fine St. Patrick's day,

But the donkey took fright at a Jersey man,
    G7   C
And started and ran away. *Chorus*

C
They both did holler with all their might
      G7   C
At the donkey for to stop.

But he upset Mary Jane, wagon and all,
       F   C
Right into a policy shop.

When McCloskey saw this cruel thing
       F   C
His heart was moved to pity

So he stabbed his donkey with a piece of charcoal,
    G7   C
And started for Salt Lake City. *Chorus*

         C
Now ladies all take warning by
G7   C
The fate of Mary Jane,

And never get into a charcoal cart,
    F   C
Unless you step out again.

The latest news from over the plain
         F   C
Comes straight from Salt Lake City:

McCloskey he has forty-five wives,
    G7   C
And is truly an object of pity. *Chorus*

The Girl I Left Behind Me

This tune was well known in Ireland before the U.S. Army (and, indeed, the U.S.) existed. The Civil War lines are given in parentheses after the Irish originals. "Alma's heights" refers to the Crimean War.

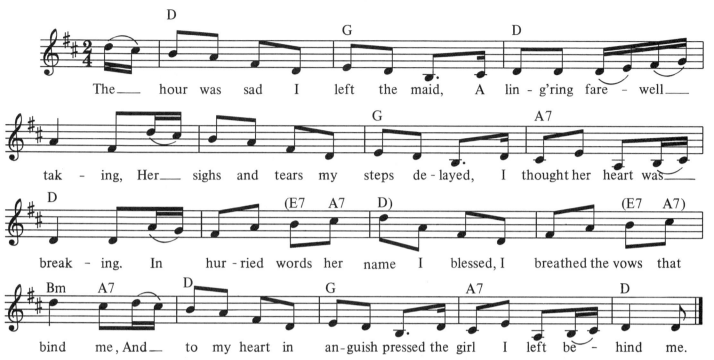

The— hour was sad I left the maid, A lin-g'ring fare-well— tak-ing, Her— sighs and tears my steps de-layed, I thought her heart was— break-ing. In hur-ried words her name I blessed, I breathed the vows that bind me, And— to my heart in an-guish pressed the girl I left be-hind me.

     D   G
Then to the East we bore away,
     D   G
(Then to the South we bore away,)
     D
To win a name in story,
              G
And there, where dawns the sun of day,
    A7   D
There dawned our sun of glory;
    (E7 A7 D)
Both blazed in noon on Alma's heights
    (E7 A7 D)
(Both blazed in noon on Freedom's height,)
    (E7 A7) Bm A7
When in the post assigned me
    D   G
I shared the glory of that fight,
     A7   D
Sweet girl I left behind me.

     D   G
Full many a name our banners bore
    D
Of former deeds of daring,
           G
But they were of the days of yore,
          G
(But they were days of Seventy-Six,)
  A7   D
In which we had no sharing;
    (E7 A7 D)
But now our laurels freshly won
      (E7 A7) Bm   A7
With the old ones shall entwined be,
    D   G
Still worthy of his sire each son,
    A7   D
Sweet girl I left behind me.

     D   G
The hope of final victory
    D
Within my bosom burning,
            G
Is mingling with sweet thoughts of thee,
   A7   D
And of my fond returning.
       (E7 A7 D)
But should I ne'er return again,
      (E7 A7) Bm A7
Still worth thy love thou'lt find me;
   D   G
Dishonor's breath shall never stain
   A7   D
The name I leave behind me.

Here is an old Irish stanza of this song - too good to leave out:

    D   G
The dames of France are fond and free,
    D
And Flemish lips are willing,
           G
And soft the maids of Italy,
     A7   D
While Spanish eyes are thrilling,
     (E7 A7 D)
Still though I bask beneath their smile,
     (E7 A7) Bm A7
Their charms quite fail to bind me,
    D   G
And my heart falls back to Erin's Isle
   A7   D
To the girl I left behind me.

Pat Murphy of the Irish Brigade

Not all Irishmen reacted to military service in the manner described in "The Seven Irishmen." During the Civil War about sixty percent of the Union army and thirty percent of the Confederate army were Irish or of Irish descent. The New York "69th" — "the Fighting Irish" — and other Irish regiments were celebrated in song, with leaders like Corcoran, Ellsworth, and Meagher.

'Twas the night be-fore bat - tle, and gath-ered in groups, The sol - diers lay close at their quar - ters; _____ A think - ing, no doubt, of their loved ones at home, of moth - ers, wives, sis - ters and daugh-ters. _____ With a pipe in his mouth sat a dash ing young blade, And a song he was sing - ing so gai - ly. _____ It was hon - est pat Mur - phy of the I - rish Bri - gade, And he sang of the sprig of shil - le - lagh. _____

(A last time)

Says Pat to his comrades, "It's a shame for to see
Brothers fightin' in such a queer manner,
But I'll fight till I die - if I shouldn't get killed,
For America's bright starry banner.
Far away in the East there's a dashing young blade,
And a song he was singin' so gaily.
'Twas honest Pat Murphy of the Irish Brigade
And the song of the splintered shillelagh.

The morning came soon and poor Paddy awoke,
On the rebels to have satisfaction.
The drummers were beatin' the devil's tattoo,
A-callin' the boys into action.
Then the Irish Brigade in the battle was seen,
And their blood for the cause shedding freely,
With their bayonet charges they rushed on the foe,
With a shout for the Land of Shillelagh.

The battle was over, the dead lay in heaps,
Pat Murphy lay bleeding and gory
A hole through his head, from a rifleman's shot
Had ended his passion for glory,
No more in the camp shall his laughter be heard,
Or the songs he was singin' so gaily.
He died like a hero, in the Land of the Free,
Far away from the Land of Shillelagh.

Now surely Columbia will never forget,
While valor and fame hold communion,
How nobly the brave Irish volunteers fought
In defense of the flag of our Union,

And if ever Old Ireland for freedom should strike,
We'll a helping hand offer quite freely.
And the Stars and the Stripes will be seen alongside
Of the flag of the Land of Shillelagh.

Irish Astronomy

By C. G. Hapline

Charles Graham Halpine (1829–1868) emigrated to America before the Civil War. He worked for a while at the *Boston Post,* and subsequently moved to New York, where he worked for the *Herald,* the *Times,* and the *Tribune.* When the war broke out he joined the "Fighting Irish" 69th Regiment, where he rose from lieutenant to brigadier general. In 1866 he became involved in an unsuccessful plot to smuggle 2,000 rifles into Ireland.

O' Ry - an was a man of might when Ire - land was a na - tion, But poach-ing was his heart's de - light and con - stant oc - cu - pa - tion He owned an old mi - li - tia gun, and cer - tain sure his aim was; He gave the keep - ers man - y a run for he did - n't care for game laws.

    E7   A   E7   F♯m E7 A
Saint Patrick once was passin' by O'Ryan's little holdin'.
        D   A   B7 E7   A   E7
And as the Saint was feelin' dry he thought he'd have a stroll in,
    A   E7   F♯m E7   A
" Ryan", said the Saint, "my son, to preach at church I'm goin'
        D   A   B7   E7   A   D E
"For God's sake let me have a rasher quick and a drop of Inishowen."

    E7   A   E7   F♯m E7   A
Says Ryan, "No rasher's good for you while better I've to spare, sir,
        D   A   B7   E7   A   E7
"But here's a jug of the mountain dew and there's a rattlin' hare sir."
       A   E7   F♯m   E7 A
Saint Patrick he looked mighty sweet, says he, "Say God attend yeh,
        D   A   B7 E7   A   D E
"And when yer in yer winding sheet it's up above I'll send yeh".

    E7   A   E7   F♯m E7   A
Bould Ryan gave his pipe a whiff—"Them tidings is transportin;
    D   A   B7 E7   A   E7
"But would yer saintship tell me if there's any kind of sporting?"
     A   E7   F♯m E7   A
Saint Patrick said, "A lion's there, two bears a bull and Cancer".
     D   A   B7   E7   A   D E
"Begod", says Mick, "The huntin's rare. Saint Paddy, I'm yer man, Sir".

    E7 A   E7   F♯m E7   A
So to conclude my song alright, for fear I'd tire your patience,
        D   A B7 E7 A   E7
You'll see O' Ryan any night amid them constellations.
      A   E7   F♯m   E7   A
And Venus follows in his tracks while Mars grows jealous daily,
       D   A   B7 E7   A   D E
But begod he fears the Irish knack of handling the shillelagh.

We've Drunk from the Same Canteen

"Private Miles O'Reilly" was actually Charles Graham Halpine. This tear jerker is right in tune with the popular sentimental ballads of the Civil War.

By "Private Miles O'Reilly"

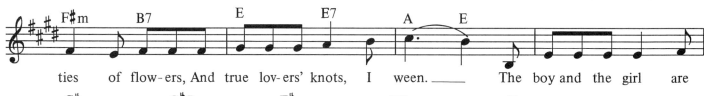

There are bonds of all sorts in this world of ours. Fet - ters of frend-ship and

ties of flow-ers, And true lov-ers' knots, I ween. ___ The boy and the girl are

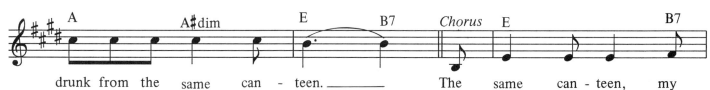

bound by a kiss, But theres nev - er a bond, ___ old friend, like this we have

drunk from the same can - teen. ___ The same can - teen, my

sol - dier friend, The same ___ can - teen. ___ There's nev-er a bond, old

friend, like this we have drunk from the same can - teen. ___

```
           E                    A
We've shared our blankets and tent together,
           E              F#m    B7
And marched and fought in all kinds of weather,
           E      E7        A E
And hungry and full we've been.
                  C#m  C#7
Had days of battle and days of rest,
         F#m     B7      E      E7
But this mem'ry I cling to and love the best,
           A        A#dim E    B7
We have drunk from the same canteen.  Chorus
```

```
           E                    A
The rich and the great sit down to dine,
            E             F#m      B7
And they quaff to each other in sparkling wine,
           E    E7        A E
From glasses crystal and green.
                   C#m          C#7
But I guess in their golden potations they miss
        F#m     B7      E      E7
The warmth of regard to be found in this
           A        A#dim E    B7
We have drunk from the same canteen.  Chorus
```

```
            E                    A
It was sometimes water, and sometimes milk,
        E              F♯m   B7
And sometimes applejack fine as silk.
        E       E7        A E
But whatever the tipple has been.
                         C♯m      C♯7
We shared it together in bane or bliss,
        F♯m         B7            E     E7
And I warm to you, friend, when I think of this
        A           A♯dim  E   B7
We have drunk from the same canteen.   Chorus
```

Last Verse

Em ... **Am** ... **B7**

For when wound-ed I lay on the out - er slope, with my blood flow-ing fast, and but

Em ... **Am** **B7**

lit - tle hope on which my faint spir - its might lean, _____ Oh,

E ... **G♯m** ... **E7**

Then, I re-mem - ber you crawled to my side, And, bleed - ing so fast it seemed

Am ... **B** ... **A** ... **A♯dim** ... **B7** ... *To Chorus*

both must have died, we drank from the same can - teen. _____

Sambo's Right to Be Kilt

Another of Charles Halpine's pseudonymous compositions. It was in his capacity as staff officer for General David Hunter that he prepared the order mustering one of the first troops of Black soldiers into the Union army. This was a highly controversial policy, and Halpine chose satire to defend his superior's actions. His song appeared in the New York *Herald* in 1862.

Words by "Private Miles O'Reilly"

Music by Samuel Lover

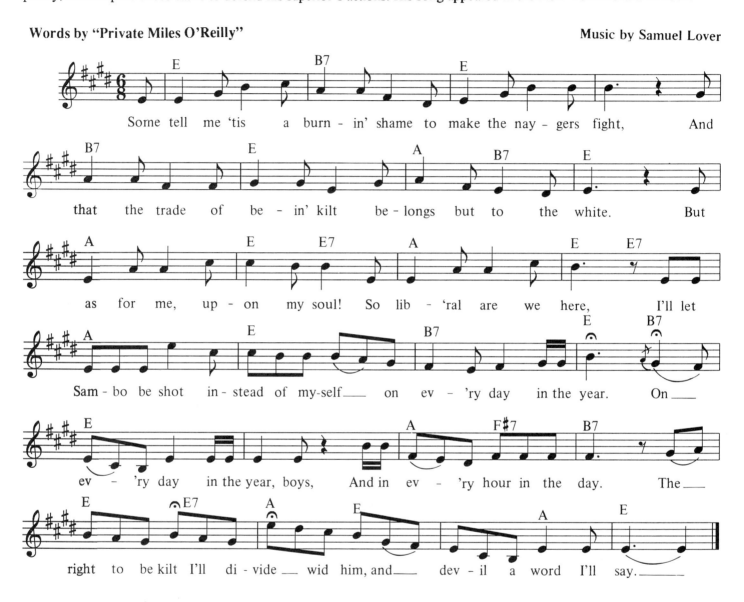

Some tell me 'tis a burn-in' shame to make the nay-gers fight, And that the trade of be-in' kilt be-longs but to the white. But as for me, up-on my soul! So lib-'ral are we here, I'll let Sam-bo be shot in-stead of my-self on ev-'ry day in the year. On ev-'ry day in the year, boys, And in ev-'ry hour in the day. The right to be kilt I'll di-vide wid him, and dev-il a word I'll say.

	E	B7
In battles wild commotion,		

E
In battles wild commotion,
E
I shouldn't at all object,
B7   E
If Sambo's body should stop a ball
A   B7 E
That's comin' for me direct;
A   E E7
And the prod of a Southern bagnet
A   E E7
So ginerous are we here,
A   E
I'll resign and let Sambo take it
B7   E
On every day in the year.
B7 E
  On ev'ry day in the year, boys,
      A   F#7 B7
  And wid none 'iv your nasty pride,
    E   E7   A   E
  All my rights in a Southern bagnet prod,
     A   E
  Wid Sambo I'll divide.

E   B7
The men who object to Sambo
E
Should take his place and fight;
B7   E
And it's better to have a nayger's hue
A   B7   E
Than a liver that's wake and white.
A   E   E7
Though Sambo's black as the ace of spades,
A   E   E7
His fingers a trigger can pull,
A   E
And his eye runs straight on the barrel sight,
B7   E
From under the thatch of wool.
B7 E
  On ev'ry day in the year, boys,
     A   F#7   B7
  Don't think that I'm tippin' you chaff,
    E   E7   A   E
  The right to be kilt we'll divide with him, boys,
       A   E
  And give him the largest half.

Then It's Irishmen, What Are You Doing?

This wonderful tune has had numerous American reincarnations. It surfaced as a campaign song for William Henry Harrison in the presidential election campaign of 1840 as "Old Tippecanoe." In 1844, as "Two Dollars a Day and Roast Beef," it helped James K. Polk defeat Henry Clay. In 1860 it really hit the big time with "Lincoln and Liberty." In 1888 it worked for Benjamin Harrison against Grover Cleveland ("Tippecanoe and Morton Too"); but, in an 1892 rewrite ("Grandfather's Hat," still trading on the memory of his grandfather, Old Tippecanoe, William Henry Harrison), it backfired—Cleveland won. Somewhere along the line it traveled out West, where as "The Old Settler's Song" it complained about the difficulties of prospecting and farming and extolled the joys of being surrounded by "acres of clams" in Puget Sound. What we have here is its 1872 version—for the losing side (Horace Greeley vs. Ulysses S. Grant). In an attempt to return to its musical roots and appeal to the Irish vote, it even "discovered" Greeley's Irish ancestry, although the first American Greeley was Zaccheus Greeley, who came from England in 1640.

D   G
It's not long ago, ye remember,
D   Bm
When Ireland was starved by a drought,
D   G
In all the whole land not a pratie
D   A7
To put in the poor children's mouth. *Chorus*

D   G
Who was it that called to the Yankees,
D   Bm
To send them a bountiful store,
D   G
'Twas the noble old man of Chappaqua,
D   A7   D
That sent over food to each door. *Chorus*

D   G
A ship, it was filled with provisions,
                  Bm
And o'er the broad sea it set sail,
D   G
'Twas the words of the man of Chappaqua,
D   A7   D
For suffering never did fail. *Chorus*

D   G
Come rally a stroke for old Greeley,
D   Bm
A stroke 'g'in corruption and fraud,
D   G
Let Irishmen rally forever,
D   A7
For Greeley, it's all come aboard. *Chorus*

D   G
When Horace is sated so snugly,
D   Bm
Way down in the White House away,
D   G
Should England git up on her ugly,
D   A7   D
You mind it, she'll just hev to pay. *Chorus*

D   G
No blood of the Cockney's in Greeley,
D   Bm
His ancestors are Irish clean through,
D   G
They've entailed a love for bright honor,
D   A7
Though born 'neath the red, white and blue. *Chorus*

D   G
Then, once again, Irishmen, rally,
D   Bm
United, my boys, just for fun,
D   G
We cannot elect a poor paddy,
D   A7   D
But only his gallant grandson. *Final Chorus*

The Regular Army, Oh!

In 1874 a version of this song appeared in sheet-music form with words by Ed Harrigan and music adapted and arranged by "Braham." The words changed to fit changing circumstances. In the Sioux campaigns of the 1870s they sang:

We're marching off for Sitting Bull,
And this is the way we go,
Forty miles a day on beans and hay
In the Regular Army, Oh!

```
        Em                        G            D
We had our choice of going to the army or to jail,
          Em                   G           D7
Or it's up the Hudson River with a copper take a sail;
              Em           G                      D
So we puckered up our courage and with bravery we did go,
            Em        C      G              Em
And we cursed the day we marched away with the Regular Army, oh!  Chorus


           Em                     G             D
When we went out to Fort Hobo they run us in the mill,
         Em                          G               D7
And there they made us take a bath, 'twas sure against our will;
             Em          G                            D
But with three full meals within our belts, each day, we had our fill,
          Em       C    G       Em
And we sat upon the dump cart and watched the terriers drill.   Chorus


          Em                    G            D
The captain's name was Murphy, of "dacint Frinch descint,"
        Em                         G          D7
Sure he knew all the holy words in the Hebrew testament;
        Em        G                        D
And when he said to Hogan, "Just move your feet a foot,"
        Em         C     G      Em
Sure Hogan jumped a half a mile on Sergeant Riley's boot.   Chorus


          Em                  G                D
The best of all the officers is Second Lieutenant McDuff;
       Em                         G            D7
Of  smoking cigarettes and sleep he never got enough.
           Em        G                           D
Says the captain, "All we want of you is to go to Reveille,
          Em          C G    Em
And we'll let the first sergeant run the company."  Chorus


        Em                    G              D
There's corns upon me feet, me boy and bunions on me toes,
          Em                         G           D7
And lugging a gun in the redhot sun puts freckles on me nose,
       Em                   G            D
And if you want a furlough to the captain you do go,
              Em          C           G        Em
And he says, "Go to bed and wait till you're dead in the Regular Army, oh!"  Chorus


        Em                  G             D
We went to Arizona for to fight the Indians there;
            Em                        G           D7
We were nearly caught baldheaded but they didn't get our hair.
      Em          G                    D
We lay among the ditches in the dirty yellow mud,
         Em        C G       Em
And we never saw an onion, a turnip, or a spud.   Chorus


            Em                    G                  D
We were captured by the Indians and brought ferninst the chafe,
        Em                      G         D7
Says he, "We'll have an Irish stew," the dirty Indian thafe,
          Em              G          D
On the telegraphic wire we skipped to Mexico,
          Em          C       G          Em
And we blessed the day we marched away from the Regular Army, oh!   Chorus
```

I'm a Roaring Repeater

"Anti-Irish sentiment was rife in the ranks of the Republican Party. . . . Nativism was a strong ideological trend in America of the 1880s. . . . The following campaign song of 1884 (Cleveland *vs.* Blaine — from the *Blaine Songster*) which purported to describe the unsavory career of an Irish hoodlum who hired himself out as a 'repeater' (i.e., a voter who voted more than once) typified the feelings of many Republicans about immigrants 'from the old sod.' " (*Songs America Voted By* by Irwin Silber)

My name is Mike Dolan, I'm one of the boys. I'm fond of good whis-key and plen-ty of noise; I'm a rare pol-i-ti-cian you'll free-ly ad-mit, Of con-science and hon-or I have not a bit, I'm called a re-peat-er, but that is my trade, I'm done with the pick-axe, the shov-el and spade, The Dem-o-crat par-ty de-pends up-on me To give them a Pres-i-dent, now don't you see.

Chorus

I'm a roar-ing re-peat-er of Dem-o-crat fame, And just from the state peni-ten-tia-ry I came, For when the e-lec-tion is com-ing a-bout, The Dem-o-crats' Gov-ern-or par-dons me out.

G
I voted for Tilden from morning till night,
C
I killed a Dutch tailor that day in a fight,
G
I scared them black fellers most out of their coats,
D7   G
And so the Republicans lost all their votes.
    D7   G
While Johnny McReady, myself and Pat Flynn,
   Am   A7   D
Stood close by the ballot-box, stuffin' them in;
D7   G
But all of our labor went up in a blaze,
   A7   D   D7
For blasted Republicans counted in Hayes. *Chorus*

Four years after that we had Hancock to lead,
C
Oh he was a jewel, a daisy indeed,
        G
And though we repeated, we couldn't do much,
D7   G
For we were outnumbered with Dutchmen and such.
    D7   G
Our beautiful Solger was left in the lurch,
   Am   A7   D
By a man from Ohio, a deacon in church;
D7   G
And so they've defeated us year after year,
   A7   D   D7
But sure there was plenty of whisky and beer. *Chorus*

O'Reilly's Gone to Hell

"Many of the old-time Irish sergeants were the finest soldiers in the (U.S.) army for twenty-five days every month, but they simply had to have their pay-day spree. . . ." (The story is told of one of these old-timers in the Philippines who, after promising his lieutenant that he would remain sober, staggered back from leave in Manila red-faced and with alcohol oozing from every pore.) "Sergeant! . . .What do you mean be breaking your word to me? . . . Didn't you tell me you were up the pole? 'Yess, sorr, lootinint . . . but shure an' 'twas a bamboo pole, sorr, an' I stopped at ivery joint!' " (*Sound Off* by Edward Arthur Dolph)

O' Reilly was a sol - dier, tle pride of Bat - t'ry B; In all the bloom-ing reg - i ment no bet - ter man than he. The rank - ing dut - y non com, he knew his bus' - ness-well; But since he tum - bled down the pole, O' Reil - lys' gone to hell.

Chorus
O' Reil - ley's gone to hell, since down the pole he fell. He drank up all the bug juice the whisk - y man would sell. They ran him in the mill. They got him in there still. His bob tail's com- ing back by mail. O' Reil - ley's gone to hell.

E   B7   E
O' Reilly hit the bottle after six years up the pole;
      F#7   B7
He blew himself at Casey's place and then went in the hole;
E   A   E
He drank with all the rookies and shoved his face as well.
A   E   B7   E
The whole outfit is on the bum. O' Reilly's gone to hell. *Chorus*

      E   B7   E
O' Reilly swiped a blanket and shoved it up, I hear;
      F#7   B7
He shoved it for a dollar and invested that in beer.
      E   A   E
He licked a coffee cooler because he said he'd tell.
      A   E   B7   E
He's ten days absent without leave. O' Reilly's gone to hell. *Chorus*

      E   B7   E
They'll try him by court martial; he'll never get a chance
      F#7   B7
To tell them how his mother **died**, or some such song and dance.
      E   A   E
He'll soon be down in Battery "Q" a sleeping in a cell,
      A   E   B7   E
A big red "P" stamped on his back. O' Reilly's gone to hell! *Chorus*

O'Donnell Aboo

Hugh Roe ("Red Hugh") O'Donnell (1572–1602) battled all his life against the English to vindicate the traditional claims of his family in north Connaught. In 1601, Phillip III of Spain, ever on the lookout for allies in Spain's perpetual hostilities against the English, sent an expeditionary force to Munster to join forces with O'Donnell. Phillip was encouraged in this action by the previous successes of Red Hugh, notably his forays in Connaught in 1595, 1597, and particularly 1599, when he defeated the English at Yellow Ford on the Blackwater. However, Phillip's expedition ended in disaster, and O'Donnell sailed off to Spain, where he died in 1602.

By H. J. McCann

Proud - ly the note of the trum - pet is sound - ing, Loud - ly the war cries a - rise on the gale. Fleet - ly the steed by Lough Swil - ly is bound - ing To join the thick squad - rons in Sam - er's green vale. On ev - 'ry moun - tain - eer! Stran gers to flight and fear; Rush to the stand - ard of daunt - less Red Hugh. Bon - noght and Gal - low - glass throng from each moun - tain pass! On for old Er - in, O' Don - nell a - boo!

| C | | | |
Princely O'Neill to our aid is advancing,
| G7 | C | D7 | G7 |
With many a chieftain and warrior-clan;
| C |
A thousand proud steeds in his vanguard are prancing,
| G | D7 | G D7 | G |
'Neath the borderers brave from the banks of the Bann.
| G7 | C |
Many a heart shall quail under the coat of mail;
| G7 | C | D7 | G7 |
Deeply the merciless foeman shall rue,
| C |
When on his ear shall ring, borne on the breeze's wing,
| G7 | C F | C |
Tirconnell's dread war-cry: O'Donnell — aboo!

| C |
Wildly o'er Desmond the war wolf is howling,
| G7 | C | D7 | G7 |
Fearless the eagle sweeps over the plain,
| C |
The fox in the streets of the city is prowling
| G | D7 | G D7 | G |
And all who would scare them are banished or slain!

| G7 | C |
Grasp, every stalwart hand, hackbut and battle-brand,
| G7 | C | D7 | G7 |
Pay them well back the deep debt so long due;
| C |
Norris and Clifford well can of Tirconnell tell.
| G7 | C F | C |
Onward to glory! O'Donnell — aboo!

| C |
Sacred the cause that Clanconnell's defending,
| G7 | C | D7 | G7 |
The altars we kneel at, the homes of our sires;
| C |
Ruthless the ruin the foe is extending,
| G | D7 | G D7 | G |
Midnight is red with the plunderer's fires!
| G7 | C |
On with O'Donnell, then, fight the old fight again;
| G7 | C | D7 | G7 |
Sons of Tirconnell all valiant and true!
| C |
Make that false Saxon feel Erin's avenging steel!
| G7 | C F | C |
Strike for your country now: O'Donnell — aboo!

O' Donnell Aboo (Abu) - Hurray for O' Donnell!

The Old Orange Flute

At the battles of the Boyne River on July 1, 1690, and at Aughrim on July 12, the Protestant army of William III (William of Orange) defeated the Catholic Irish army of James II (James Stuart). In the rancor that followed their defeat, James called his followers cowards. There was a strong difference of opinion as to who was really the coward — and James was repaid with the opprobrious nickname of "Seamus-a-Cacagh," or dirty (sic) James. The anniversary of these battles is celebrated each year in Northern Ireland, however. This song — with its gentle good humor — is sung throughout Ireland.

In the coun - ty Ty - rone near the town of Dun - gan - non, where many the ruc - tions me - self had a han' - in, Bob Wil - liam - son lived, a weav - er by trade, and all of us thought him a stout Or - ange blade. On the twelfth of Ju - ly as it year - ly did come, Bob played with his flute to the sound of a drum. You many talk of your harp, your pi - an - o, or lute, but there's none can com - pare with the old Or - ange flute.

C   G7 C
Now Bob, the deceiver, he took us all in,
      D7   G7
He married a Papist named Bridget McGinn,
    C   Em   F   C
Turned Papish himself, and forsook the old cause,
       F   G7   C
That gave us our freedom, religion, and laws.
    C7   F
Now the boys the place made some comment upon it,
 C   G7
And Bob had to fly to the province of Connaught,
 C   Em   F   C
He fled with his wife and his fixings to boot,
      F   G7   C
And along with the latter, his old Orange flute.

    C   G7   C
At the chapel on Sunday to atone for past deeds,
      D7   G7
Said *paters* and *aves* and counted his beads,
   C   Em   F   C
'Til after some time at the priest's own desire,
       F   G7   C
He went with the old flute to play in the choir.
   C7   F
He went with the old flute for to play for the mass,
  C   G7
But the instrument shivered, and sighed, oh, alas,
  C   Em   F   C
And try though he would, though it made a great noise,
     F   G7   C
The flute would play only "The Protestant Boys."

    C   G7   C
Bob jumped and he started and got in a flutter;
      D7   G7
And threw the old flute in the blessed holy water,
    C   Em   F   C
He thought that this charm would bring some other sound,
     F   G7   C
When he tried it again, it played "Croppies Lie Down."
    C7   F
Now for all he could whistle and finger and blow,
  C   G7
To play Papish music he found it no go,
      C   Em   F   C
"Kick the Pope," and "Boil Water" it freely would sound,
       F   G7   C
But one Papish squeak in it couldn't be found.

    C   G7   C
At the council of priests that was held the next day,
      D7   G7
They decided to banish the old flute away,
    C   Em F   C
They couldn't knock heresy out of its head,
       F   G7
So they bought Bob a new one to play in its stead.
    C7   F
Now the old flute was doomed, and its fate was pathetic,
   C   G7
'Twas fastened and burned at the stake as heretic,
    C   Em   F   C
As the flames soared around it, they heard a strange noise,
     F   G7   C
'Twas the old flute still whistling "The Protestant Boys."

Clare's Dragoons

The "Wild Geese" — Irishmen fighting in foreign armies (often against England) — distinguished themselves many times over in battle. At the battle of Fontenoy in May 1745, their heroic actions helped turn the tide against the English, causing George II to exclaim: "Cursed be the laws which deprive me of such subjects!" The battle of Ramillies, also in Belgium, took place exactly thirty-nine years earlier, in May 1706. Despite the bravado of the song it was the Duke of Marlborough who defeated the French.

When __ on Ram - il - lies' blood - y field, The baf - fled French were forced __ to __ yield, The vic - tor Sax - on back — ward reeled be - fore the charge of Clare's dra - goons. The flags we con - quered in that fray, Look lone in Yp - res' choir __ they __ say, We'll win them com - pan - y to-day, Or brave - ly die like Clare's dra - goons. Then __ vi - va la, for Ire - lands wong! __ Vi - va la, for Ire __ land's __ right! Then vi - va - la, in bat - tle throngh, For a Span-ish steed and sa - ber bright!

A
Another Clare is here to lead,
D
Tho worthy son of such a breed;
A
The French expect some famous deed,
D   E7   A
When Clare leads on his bold dragoons.
E7   A
Our colonel comes from Brian's race,
A7   D
His wounds are in his breast and face,
A   C#7   F#m   Dm
The *bearna baoghail* is still his place,
A   D   E7   A
The foremost of his bold dragoons. *Chorus*

A
Oh! comrades, think how Ireland pines,
D
Her exiled lords, her rifled shrines,
A
Her dearest hope, the ordered lines,
D   E7   A
And bursting charge of Clare's dragoons.
E7   A
Then fling your green flag to the sky,
A7   D
Be *Limerick!* your battle-cry,
A   C#7   F#m   Dm
And charge, till blood floats fetlock high
A   D   E7   A
Around the track of Clare's dragoons.

Final Chorus

Then, viva la, the new brigade!
D
Viva la, the old one too!
A   C#7   F#m
Then, viva la, the rose shall fade,
Dm   A   D   E7 A
And the shamrock shine forever new!

bearna baoghail (pr. barna bwail): literally, the gap of danger — that is, wherever there is danger.

The Wearing of the Green

James Napper Tandy (1740–1803) was born in Dublin. During the 1780s and '90s he was actively involved in Irish revolutionary causes. He helped found the Society of United Irishmen with Wolfe Tone, and became its first secretary in 1791. Greatly influenced by the French Revolution, and with French naval support, he helped lead an unsuccessful invasion from Dunkirk to Donegal in September 1798. After fleeing to Hamburg via Scotland and Norway he was extradited to England, where he was imprisoned until 1801 under sentence of death. He was eventually released, due in part to the vigorous intervention on his behalf by Bonaparte.

Then if the color we must wear is England's cruel red,
$$D \qquad E7 \qquad A$$
Sure Ireland's sons shall ne'er forget the blood that they have shed.
$$G \qquad D \qquad G \qquad D$$
You may take the shamrock from your hat and cast it on the sod;
$$E7 \qquad A$$
But 'twill take root and flourish there, though underfoot 'tis trod.
$$G \qquad D \qquad G \qquad D$$
When laws can stop the blades of grass from growin' as they grow,
$$A7 \qquad D$$
And when the leaves in summertime, their verdure dare not show,
$$E7 \qquad A$$
Then I will change the color that I wear in my caubeen,
$$D \qquad E7 \qquad A$$
But till that day, please God, I'll stick to wearin' of the green.
$$G \qquad D \qquad G \qquad D$$

The Croppy Boy

"The term Croppy has a much-disputed derivation, some referring it to the cropped ears of convicted felons (any political action was felony in Ireland), some to the pitch-cap torture applied to rebels, others to the 'democratic' haircut favoured by the supporters of the French Revolution, others to the fact that only the lower orders wore their hair short, and others to the ancient Gaelic Irish hair style of a short square-cut bob with a fringe. The probability is that the term includes all of these connotations, since all of them are factually applicable to the rebel patriot Irish." (Patrick Galvin, *Irish Songs of Resistance*)

It was ear - ly ear - ly _____ in the spring, The birds did whis-tle_____ and__ sweet - ly sing. Chang-ing their notes from _ tree to tree, And the song they sang____ was Old Ire - land free.

G   C
It was early, early in the night,
 D7   G
The yeoman cavalry gave me a fright;
     Am D7 Em
The yeoman cavalry was my downfall,
  Am D7 G
And I was taken by Lord Cornwall.

G   C
As I was passing my father's door,
 D7   G
My brother William stood at the door.
     Am D7 Em
My aged father stood at the door;
   Am D7 G
And my tender mother her hair she tore.

G   C
As I was going up Wexford Street,
 D7   G
My own first cousin I chanced to meet;
     Am D7 Em
My own first cousin did me betray,
   Am   D7 G
And for one bare guinea swore my life away.

G   C
As I was walking up Wexford **Hill,**
D7   G
Who could blame me to cry my fill?
     Am D7 Em
I looked behind and I looked before,
    Am D7 G
But my aged mother I shall ne'er see more.

G   C
'Twas in the guardhouse where I was laid
 D7   G
And in a parlor where I was tried;
     Am D7 Em
My sentence passed and my courage low
  Am   D7 G
When to Dungannon I was forced to go,

G   C
As I was mounted on the platform high,
 D7   G
My aged father was standing by;
     Am D7 Em
My aged father did me deny,
   Am   D7 G
And the name he gave me was the Croppy Boy.

   G   C
It was in Dungannon this young man died
   D7   G
And in Dungannon his body lies;
       Am D7 Em
And you good people that do pass by,
   Am   D7   G
Oh, shed a tear for the Croppy Boy.

The Shan Van Vocht

One of the many "code names" for Ireland, The Shan Van Vocht means "The Little Old Lady." French General Lazare Hoche led an invasion force toward Ireland in December 1796. Wolfe Tone had persuaded the French to mount this attack. They arrived in Bantry Bay on Christmas, but a terrible tempest arose and dispersed the French fleet. Hoche became separated from the rest of the expedition and, in great confusion, the whole fleet returned to Brest.

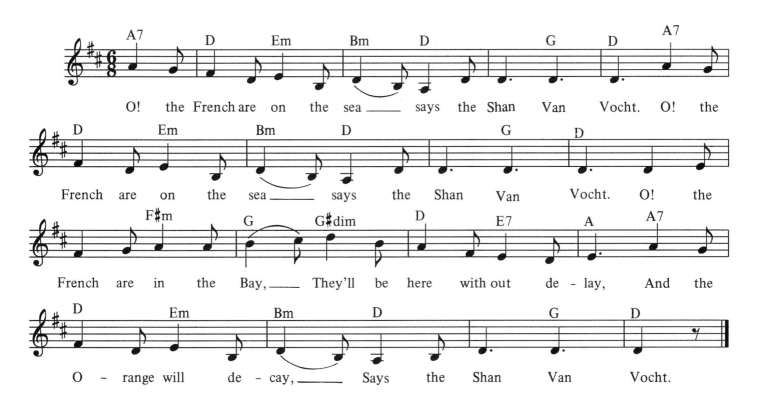

A7   D   Em   Bm
And where will they have their camp?
D   G   D
Says the Shan Van Vocht;
 A7 D   Em   Bm
Where will they have their camp?
D   G   D
Says the Shan Van Vocht;
       F♯m   G
On the Curragh of Kildare,
G♯dim   D E7   A
The boys they will be there,
 A7   D   Em Bm
With their pikes in good repair,
  D   G   D
Says the Shan Van Vocht.

A7   D   Em   Bm
And what colour will they wear?
D   G   D
Says the Shan Van Vocht;
A7 D   Em   D
What colour will they wear?
          G   D
Says the Shan Van Vocht;
         F♯m   G
What colour should be seen
G♯dim   D E7   A
Where our fathers' homes have been,
 A7   D   Em   Bm
But their own immortal green?
  D   G   D
Says the Shan Van Vocht.

    A7   D   Em   Bm
And will Ireland then be free?
D   G   D
Says the Shan Van Vocht;
A7 D Em   Bm
Will Ireland then be free?
D   G   D
Says the Shan Van Vocht;
        F♯m   G
Yes! Ireland shall be free
G♯dim   D E7   A
From the center to the sea;
  A7 D   Em Bm
Then hurrah for Liberty!
  D   G   D
Says the Shan Van Vocht.

The Patriot Mother

The "pikes of Curragh" are mentioned in "The Shan Van Vocht."

Words by Mary Eva Kelly
Tune: Mountains of Mourne

"Come tell us the name of the re-bel-ly crew who lift-ed the pike on the Cur-ragh with you, Come
tell us the trea-son and then you'll be free, or quick-ly you'll swing from the high gal-lows tree, "A-lan-na! A-lan-na! the shad-ow of shame has nev-er yet fal-len on one of your name. And o, may the food from my bos-om you drew, In your veins turn to poi-son, if you turn un-true.

G   C
"The foul words, O let them not blacken your tongue,
D7   G
That would prove to your friends and your country a wrong,
        C
Or the curse of a mother, so bitter and dread,
  D7   G
With the wrath of the **Lord,** may they fall on your head.
D7   G
I have no one but you in the whole world wide.
    E7   A7 D7
Yet false to your pledge, you'd ne'er stand at my side.
G B7   C **C♯dim**
If a traitor you lived you'd be farther away
D7   Gsus4   G
From my heart than, if true, you were wrapped in the clay."

G   C
"O deeper and darker the mourning would be,
D7   G
For your falsehood so base, than your death proud and free.
        C
Dearer, far dearer than ever to me,
  D7   G
My darling, you'll be on the brave gallows tree.
  D7   G
'Tis holy, agra, from the bravest and best
    E7   A7   D7
Go! go! from my heart and be joined with the rest,
  G B7 C **C♯dim**
Alanna machree! O alanna machree!
  D7   Gsus4 G
Sure a cowardly traitor you never would be."

      G   C
There's no look of traitor upon the young brow
    D7   G
That's raised to the tempters so haughtily now;
       C
No traitor e'er held up the firm head so high —
   D7   G
No traitor e'er showed such a proud flashing eye.
    D7   G
On the high gallows tree! on the brave gallows tree!
     E7   A7   D7
Where smiled leaves and blossoms, his sad doom met he.
   G B7 C **C♯dim**
But it never bore blossom so pure and so fair
    D7   Gsus4   G
As the heart of the martyr that hangs from it there.

Father Murphy

In November 1797 Father John Murphy and nine other priests voluntarily swore allegiance to George III, denied on oath that they were members of the Society of United Irishmen, and swore to give information against the rebels. Their parishes soon followed suit, Boulavogue in County Wexford taking the oath on April 9, 1798. This was a tactic to allay suspicion, for on May 26 Father Murphy lit the beacon fire on Corrigua Hill, signaling the uprising. Lord Caslereagh, Chief Secretary for Ireland, wrote on June 12: "The priests lead the rebels to battle . . . and show the most desperate resolution in their attack. . . . It is a Jacobinical conspiracy."

By P. J. McCall

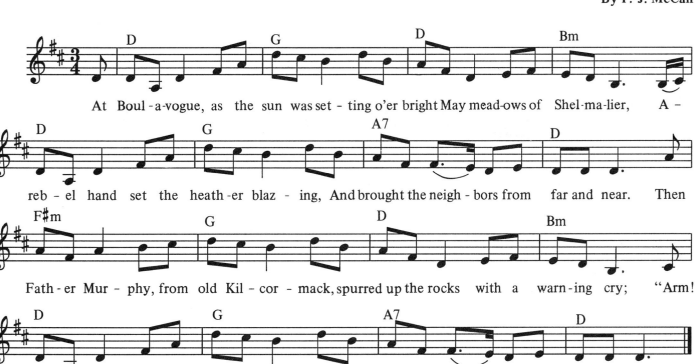

At Boul-a-vogue, as the sun was set-ting o'er bright May mead-ows of Shel-ma-lier, A-

reb-el hand set the heath-er blaz-ing, And brought the neigh-bors from far and near. Then

Fath-er Mur-phy, from old Kil-cor-mack, spurred up the rocks with a warn-ing cry; "Arm!

Arm!" he cried, "for I've come to lead you, For Ire-land's free-dom we fight or die."

D		G
He led us on 'gainst the coming soldiers,
D		Bm
The cowardly Yeomen we put to flight;
D		G
'Twas at the Harrow the boys of Wexford
| | A7 | D |
Showed Bookey's regiment how men could fight.
| F#m | | G |
Look out for hirelings, King George of England,
| D | | Bm |
Search every kingdom where breathes a slave,
| D | | G |
For Father Murphy of the County Wexford
| A7 | | D |
Sweeps o'er the land like a mighty wave.

D		G
We took Camolin and Enniscorthy,
D		Bm
And Wexford storming drove out our foes;
D		G
'Twas at Slieve Coillte our pikes were reeking
| | A7 | D |
With the crimson stream of the beaten Yeos.
| F#m | | G |
At Tubberneering and Ballyellis
| D | | Bm |
Full many a Hessian lay in his gore;
| D | | G |
Ah, Father Murphy, had aid come over,
| A7 | | D |
The green flag floated from shore to shore!

D		G
At Vinegar Hill, o'er the pleasant Slaney,
D		Bm
Our heroes vainly stood back to back,
D		G
And the Yeos at Tullow took Father Murphy
A7		D
And burned his body upon the rack.
F#m		G
God grant you glory, brave Father Murphy,
D		Bm
And open Heaven to all your men;
D		G
The cause that called you may call tomorrow
A7		D
In another fight for the green again.

Roddy McCorley

Undaunted by the disaster of the 1796 unsuccessful invasion attempt (referred to in "The Shan Van Vocht"), Wolfe Tone tried again in 1798. This time he was captured by the British when his French man-o'-war was forced to surrender. Condemned to be hanged, he died of self-inflicted wounds before the sentence could be carried out (November 19, 1798). For his part in the uprising, Roddy McCorley, a young patriot, was hanged in Toomebridge, County Antrim.

By Ethna Carbery

Ho, — see the fleet foot — hosts of men, — who speed with fac - es wan; From — farm - stead and from — fish - er's cot up - on the banks of Bann. They — come with venge - ance — in their eyes, Too late, too late are they, For young Rod - dy M' - Cor - ley — goes to die on the Bridge of Toome to - day.

G
Up the narrow street he stepped,
C   G
Smiling and proud and young;
            C   G
About the hemp-rope on his neck
    C   Am   D7
The golden ringlets clung.
       G   C   G
There's never a tear in his blue eyes,
   Em   Am   D7
Both glad and bright are they -
      G
As young Roddy M'Corley goes to die
    C   (Cm)G
On the Bridge of Toome today.

G
When he last stepped up that street
         C   G
His shining pike in hand,
             C   G
Behind him marched in grim array
    C   Am   D7
A stalwart earnest band!
    G   C   G
For Antrim town! for Antrim town!
   Em   Am   D7
He led them to the fray -
       G
And young Roddy M'Corley goes to die
    C   (Cm) G
On the Bridge of Toome today.

           G
There is never a one of all your dead
       C   G
More bravely fell in fray,
            C   G
Then he who marches to his fate
      C   Am   D7
On the Bridge of Toome today.

G   C   G
True to the last, true to the last,
   Em   Am   D7
He treads the upward way -
       G
And young Roddy M'Corley goes to die
    C   (Cm) G
On the Bridge of Toome today.

The Men of the West

In August 1798, the French under General J.J. Humbert landed in County Mayo and, aided by a popular uprising, defeated the English at Castlebar. But they could not prevail, and were finally crushed by superior numbers.

By William Rooney

When you hon or in song and in stor - y the names of the pat - ri - ot men ___ Whose
va - lor has cov-ered with glo - ry full man - y a moun-tain and glen, ___ . For -
get not the boys of the heath - er who mar-shalled the brav-est and best, ___ When
Ire - land was bro - ken in Wex - ford and looked for re - venge to the west. ___

Chorus
I give you the gal - lant old West, boys Where ral - lied our brav-est and best, ___ When
Ire - land lay bro -ken and bleed - ing; Hur - rah for the men of the West! ___

| D | G | D | Bm |
The hilltops with glory were glowing, 'twas the eve of a bright harvest day
| D | G | D | A7 | D |
When the ships we'd been wearily waiting sailed into Killala's broad bay.
| G | D | Bm |
And over the hill went the slogan, to awaken in every breast
| D | G | D | A7 | D |
The fire that has never been quenched, boys, among the true hearts of the West. *Chorus*

| D | G | D | Bm |
Killala was ours 'ere the midnight, and high over Ballina town
| D | G | D | A7 | D |
Our banners in triumph were waving before the next sun had gone down.
| G | D | Bm |
We gathered to speed the good work, boys, the true men from near and afar;
| D | G | D | A7 | D |
And history can tell how we routed the redcoats through old Castlebar. *Chorus*

| D | G | D | Bm |
And pledge me the stout sons of France, boys, bold Humbert and all his brave men,
| D | G | D | A7 | D |
Whose tramp, like the trumpet of battle, brought hope to the drooping again.
| G | D | Bm |
Since Ireland has caught to her bosom on many a mountain and hill
| D | G | D | A7 | D |
The gallants who fell, so they're here, boys, to cheer us to victory still. *Chorus*

| D | G | D | Bm |
Though all the bright dreamings we cherished went down in disaster and woe,
| D | G | D | A7 | D |
The spirit of old is still with us that never would bend to the foe;
| G | D | Bm |
And Connaught is ready whenever the loud rolling tuck of the drum
| D | G | D | A7 | D |
Rings out to awaken the echoes and tell us the morning has come.

Final Chorus
| D | G |
So here's to the gallant old West, boys,
| D | Bm |
Who rallied her bravest and best
| D | G |
When Ireland was broken and bleeding;
| D | A7 | D |
Hurrah! for the men of the West!

93

Kelly, the Boy from Killann

Another song of the 1798 Rebellion—this one from County Wexford. Bargy and Shelmalier are baronies in Wexford. Baronies are subdivisions of counties that were formed out of the territories of the Irish chiefs as each submitted to English rule.

By P. J. McCall

1. Tell me who is the giant with the gold curling hair,
He who rides at the head of your band.
Seven feet is his height with some inches to spare,
And he looks like a king in command.
O my boys that's the pride of the bold Shelmaliers,
'Mongst our greatest of heroes, a man.
Fling your beavers aloft and give three ringing cheers
For John Kelly, the boy from Killann.

2. Enniscorthy's in flames and old Wexford is won,
And the Barrow tomorrow we will cross.
On the hill o'er the town we have planted a gun
That will batter the gateway to Ross.
All the Forth men and Bargy men march o'er the heath,
With brave Harvey to lead in the van;
But the foremost of all in the grim gap of death,
Will be Kelly, the boy from Killann.

3. But the gold sun of freedom grew darkened at Ross,
And it set by the Slaney's red waves.
And poor Wexford stripped naked hung high on a cross,
With her heart pierced by traitors and slaves.
Glory-o, Glory-o to her brave sons who died
For the cause of long down trodden man.
Glory-o to Mount Leinster's own darling and pride,
Dauntless Kelly, the boy from Killann.

94

The Rising of the Moon

In suppressing the Rebellion of 1798, and all the other uprisings before and after that date, England was merely following the advice expressed in this poem, written in 1436:

> Nowe here beware and hertly take entente,
> As we woll answere at the last jugemente,
> To kepen Irelond, that it not be loste,
> For it is a boterasse and a poste
> Undre England and Wales is another,
> God forbede but sche were other brothere,
> Of one ligeaunce dewe until the kynge.

By John Keegan Casey

"Oh! then tell me, Sean O'-Far-rell, tell me why you hur-ry so?"

"Hush, a while, just hush and lis-ten," and his cheeks were all a-glow.

"I bear or-ders— from the Cap-tain, get you read-y quick and soon,

For the pikes must be to-geth-er at the ris-ing of the moon!"

Dm   F Dm C Bb Am
"Oh! then tell me, Sean O' Farrell, where the gathering is to be?"
Dm   F   Am C Dm
"In the old spot by the river, right well known to you and me.
         C Am Dm F Bb   Am
One word more - for signal token – whistle up the marching tune,
Dm   F   Am C Dm
With your pike upon your shoulder, by the rising of the moon."

Dm   F Dm   C Bb   Am
Out from many a mudwall cabin eyes were watching through the night,
Dm   F   Am C Dm
Many a manly breast was throbbing for the blessed warning light.
        C Am Dm F Bb Am
Murmurs passed along the valley, like the banshee's lonely croon,
Dm   F   Am C Dm
And a thousand blades were flashing at the rising of the moon.

Dm   F Dm C Bb   Am
There beside the singing river that dark mass of men were seen,
Dm   F   Am C Dm
Far above the shining weapons hung their own immortal green.
        C Am Dm F Bb   Am
"Death to every foe and traitor! Forward! Strike the marching tune,
Dm   F   Am C Dm
And, hurrah, my boys, for freedom! 'tis the rising of the moon."

Bold Robert Emmet

Robert Emmet (1778–1803) was born in Dublin. As a student at Trinity College, he showed great promise of a distinguished academic career, but he removed his name from the college books in April 1798 as a protest against the inquisitorial examination of the political views of the students conducted by the chancellor of the university. He then turned his full attention toward political activism. After the disastrous uprising of 1798, he travelled to France, where he met with other members of the rebellion who were planning another attempt. In October 1802 he had an interview with Bonaparte, which convinced him that a French invasion of England might be expected in August 1803. However, the plan miscarried when the British got wind of the plot. Forced into premature action, and without French assistance, the uprising ended in confusion and disaster. Emmet was captured and hanged on September 20, 1803.

The strug-gle is o-ver, the boys are de-feat-ed old
Hung, drawn, and quar-tered, sure that was my sen-tence; But

Ire-land's sur-round-ed with sad-ness and gloom, We were de-
soon I will show them no cow-ard am I. My crime is the

feat-ed and shame-ful-ly treat-ed, And I, Rob-ert Em-met, a-
love of the land I was born in, A he-ro I lived and a

wait now my doom. *Chorus* Bold Rob-ert Em-met, the dar-ling of Ire-land,
he-ro I'll die,

Bold Rob-ert Em-met will die with a smile. Fare-well, com-pan-ions both

loy-al and dar-ing, I'll lay down my life— for the Em-er-ald Isle.

G	C	G

The barque lay at anchor awaiting to bring me
Em   A7   D7
Over the billows to the land of the free;
G   C   G
But I must see my sweetheart for I know she will cheer me,
C   G   D7   G
And with her I will sail far over the sea.
C   G
But I was arrested and cast into prison,
Em   A7   D7
Tried as a traitor, a rebel, a spy;
G   C   G
But no man can call me a knave or a coward,
C   G   D7   G
A hero I lived and a hero I'll die. *Chorus*

G   C   G
Hark! the bell's tolling, I well know its meaning,
Em   A7   D7
My poor heart tells me it is my death knell;
G   C   G
In come the clergy, the warder is leading,
C   G   D7   G
I have no friends here to bid me farewell.
C   G
Goodbye, old Ireland, my parents and sweetheart,
Em   A7   D7
Companions in arms to forget you must try;
G   C   G
I am proud of the honour, it was only my duty
C   G   D7   G
A hero I lived and a hero I'll die. *Chorus*

The Bonny Bunch of Roses

This version of this song, which is undoubtedly of English origin, comes from Dungannon in County Tyrone. The "bonny bunch of roses" is, of course, England; but the "Emmet–Bonaparte connection" (described in "Bold Robert Emmet") makes this song doubly interesting and significant here.

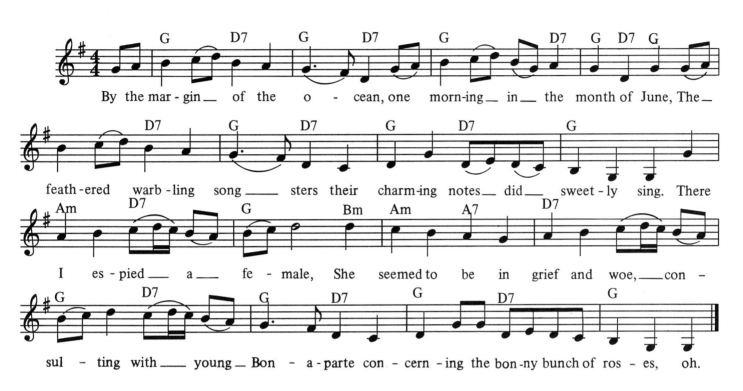

By the mar-gin __ of the o - cean, one morn-ing __ in __ the month of June, The __ feath-ered warb-ling song _____ sters their charm-ing notes __ did __ sweet-ly sing. There I es - pied __ a __ fe - male, She seemed to be in grief and woe, ___ con - sul - ting with ___ young __ Bon - a - parte con - cern - ing the bon -ny bunch of ros - es, oh.

G   D7   G D7   G   D7 G D7 G
Then up steps young Napoleon and takes his mother by the hand,
           D7   G D7 G   D7   G
Saying, "Mother dear, have patience until I'm able to take command.
   Am   D7   G   Bm Am   A7   D7
I'll raise a terrible army, and through tremendous dangers go,
     G   D7   G D7   G   D7
And in spite of all the universe, I will conquer the bonny bunch of
 G
roses, oh.

        G   D7   G   D7   G   D7 G D7
The first time I saw young Napoleon, down on his bended knee fell
 G
he,
        D7   G D7   G   D7   G
He asked the pardon of his father, who granted it most mournfully.
   Am   D7   G Bm Am   A7 D7
"Dear son," he said, "I'll take an army, and over the frozen Alps will
go,
  G   D7 G D7   G   D7   G
Then I will conquer Moscow, and return to the bonny bunch of roses,
oh."

        G   D7   G   D7   G   D7   G D7
He took five hundred-thousand men, with kings likewise to bear his
 G
train,
                D7   G   D7   G   D7   G
He was so well provided for that he could sweep the world alone.
       Am   D7   G   Bm Am A7   D7
But when he came to Moscow, he was overpowered by the driven
snow,
            G   D7   G D7   G   D7   G
When Moscow was a-blazing, so he lost his bonny bunch of roses,
oh.

        G   D7   G   D7   G   D7   G
"Oh son, don't speak so venturesome, for in England are the hearts
D7 G
of oak.
                  D7   G D7   G D7   G
There is England, Ireland, Scotland — their unity was never broke.
       Am   D7 G   Bm Am   A7   D7
Oh son, think on thy father, on the Isle of St. Helena his body lies low,
         G   D7 G D7   G   D7
And you may soon follow after him — so beware of the bonny bunch
 G
of roses, oh."

            G   D7   G D7   G   D7 G D7 G
"Now do believe me dearest mother — now I lie on my dying bed,
               D7   G D7 G   D7   G
If I'd lived I would have been cleverer, but now I droop my youthful head.
          Am   D7   G   Bm Am   A7   D7
But whilst our bodies lie mouldering, and weeping willows over our bodies grow,
        G   D7 G D7   G   D7   G
The deeds of great Napoleon shall sing the bonny bunch of roses, oh."

John Mitchel

"We must go to countries like the Asiatic provinces of Turkey, devastated by Ottoman rule, to find such a diminution in the numbers of people as was seen in Ireland during the last half of the 19th century. A terrible series of agrarian crimes was committed in the summer of 1847; and the ministry felt compelled . . . to strengthen its hands by . . . suspending the Habeas Corpus Act in Ireland. The latter measure at once brought to a crisis the so-called rebellion of 1848. . . . The government . . . introduced an act enabling it to commute the death penalty to transportation. The insurrection had from the first proved abortive. With . . . transportion it practically terminated." (*Encyclopedia Britannica*, Vol. IX, 1911 edition)

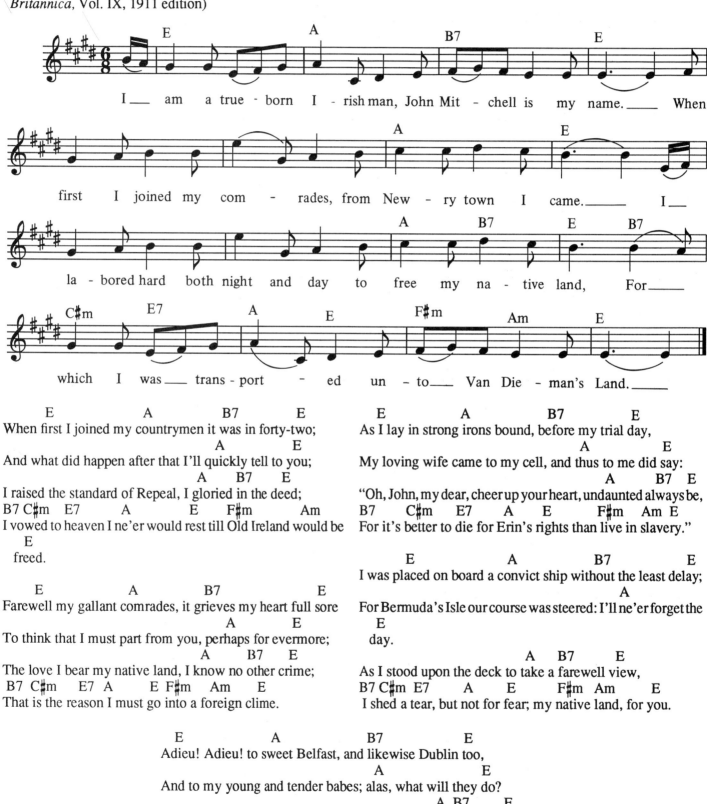

          E   A   B7   E

I am a true-born Irishman, John Mitchell is my name. When

first I joined my comrades, from Newry town I came. I

labored hard both night and day to free my native land, For

which I was transported unto Van Dieman's Land.

E	A	B7	E

When first I joined my countrymen it was in forty-two;
                                A   E
And what did happen after that I'll quickly tell to you;
                       A   B7   E
I raised the standard of Repeal, I gloried in the deed;
B7 C#m E7   A   E   F#m   Am
I vowed to heaven I ne'er would rest till Old Ireland would be
  E
  freed.

      E   A   B7   E
Farewell my gallant comrades, it grieves my heart full sore
                          A   E
To think that I must part from you, perhaps for evermore;
                   A   B7   E
The love I bear my native land, I know no other crime;
B7 C#m   E7 A   E F#m Am   E
That is the reason I must go into a foreign clime.

E	A	B7	E

As I lay in strong irons bound, before my trial day,
                                 A   E
My loving wife came to my cell, and thus to me did say:
                                     A   B7   E
"Oh, John, my dear, cheer up your heart, undaunted always be,
B7   C#m   E7   A   E   F#m Am E
For it's better to die for Erin's rights than live in slavery."

                   E   A   B7   E
I was placed on board a convict ship without the least delay;
                                      A
For Bermuda's Isle our course was steered: I'll ne'er forget the
  E
  day.
                                A B7   E
As I stood upon the deck to take a farewell view,
B7 C#m E7   A   E   F#m Am   E
I shed a tear, but not for fear; my native land, for you.

                   E   A   B7   E
Adieu! Adieu! to sweet Belfast, and likewise Dublin too,
                                A   E
And to my young and tender babes; alas, what will they do?
                                A B7   E
But there's one request I ask of you, when your liberty you gain
B7 C#m   E7   A E   F#m Am   E
Remember John Mitchel far away, though a convict bound in chains.

The Praties, They Grow Small

The exotic potato was introduced into Ireland by Sir Walter Raleigh. By the 18th century, potatoes and buttermilk made up the diet of the poor. A British official wrote, "What hope is there for a nation that lives on potatoes!" In 1844 a hitherto unknown disease attacked the North American potato crop. The blight soon made itself felt in Ireland with devastating results. The winter of 1846–47 was "the most severe in living memory." There were great icy gales blowing "perfect hurricanes of snow, hail and sleet." And there was nothing to eat. In January 1847 W. E. Forster wrote that Westport in Mayo was "a strange and fearful sight, like what we read of in beleaguered cities, the streets crowded with gaunt wanderers . . . walking skeletons, the men stamped with the livid mark of hunger, the children crying with pain, the women in some of the cabins, too weak to stand. . . ."

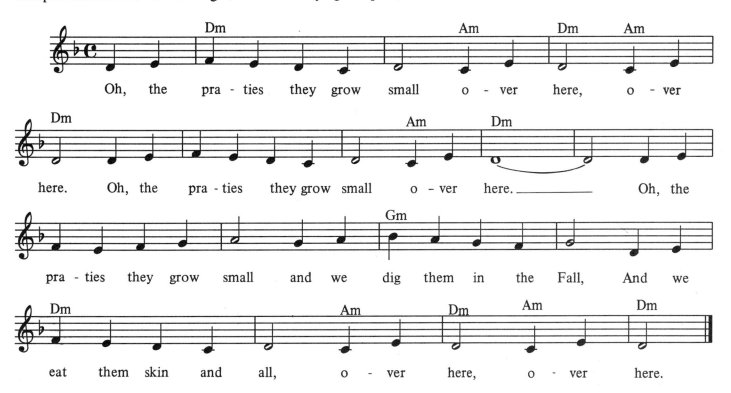

Oh, the pra-ties they grow small o-ver here, o-ver here. Oh, the pra-ties they grow small o-ver here. Oh, the pra-ties they grow small and we dig them in the Fall, And we eat them skin and all, o-ver here, o-ver here.

Dm
Oh, I wish that we were geese,
Am   Dm   Am   Dm
Night and morn, night and morn.

Oh, I wish that we were geese,
Am   Dm
Night and morn.

Oh, I wish that we were geese,
Gm
For they fly and take their ease,
Dm
And they live and die in peace,
Am   Dm   Am   Dm
Eating corn, eating corn.

Dm
Oh, we're trampled in the dust,
Am Dm   Am Dm
Over here, over here.

Oh, we're trampled in the dust,
Am Dm
Over here.

Oh, we're trampled in the dust,
Gm
But the Lord in whom we trust
Dm
Will give us crumb for crust,
Am Dm   Am Dm
Over here, over here.

99

Skibbereen

"My Lord Duke . . . I went on the 15th instant to Skibbereen, and . . . I shall state simply what I there saw. . . . Being aware that I should have to witness scenes of frightful hunger, I provided myself with as much bread as five men could carry, and on reaching the spot I was surprised to find the wretched hamlet deserted. I entered some of the hovels to ascertain the cause, and the scenes which presented themselves were such as no tongue or pen can convey the slightest idea of. In the first, six famished and ghastly skeletons, to all appearances dead, were huddled in a corner. . . . I approached with horror, and found by a low moaning they were alive — they were in a fever, four children, a woman and what had once been a man. . . . In a few minutes I was surrounded by at lest 200 such phantoms, such frightful spectres as no words can describe, either from famine or from fever. . . ." (Excerpt of a letter from Nicholas Cummins, magistrate of Cork to the Duke of Wellington, published in *The Times*, December 24, 1846.)

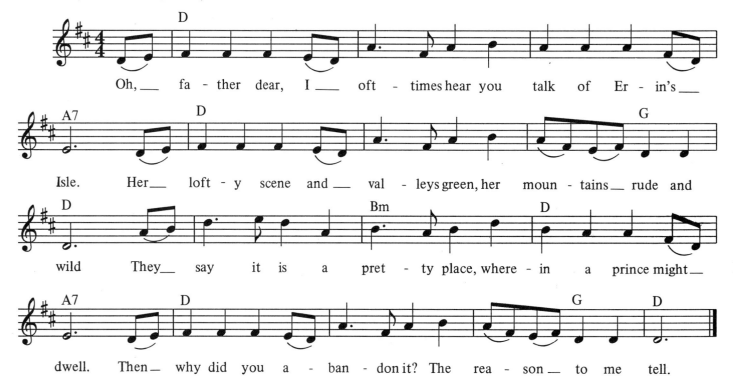

Oh, __ fa - ther dear, I __ oft - times hear you talk of Er - in's __ Isle. Her __ loft - y scene and __ val - leys green, her moun - tains __ rude and wild They __ say it is a pret - ty place, where - in a prince might __ dwell. Then __ why did you a - ban - don it? The rea - son __ to me tell.

D	A7
My son, I loved our native land with energy and pride,
D		G D
Until a blight came on the land, and sheep and cattle died.
Bm	D	A7
The rent and taxes were to pay, I could not them redeem,
D		G D
And that's the cruel reason why I left old Skibbereen.

| D | A7 |
It's well I do remember the year of forty-eight,
| D | | G D |
When I arose with Erin's boys to fight against the fate,
| Bm | D | A7 |
I was hunted through the mountains for a traitor to the Queen.
| D | | G D |
And that's another reason why I left old Skibbereen.

| D | A7 |
It's well I do remember that black December day,
| D | | G D |
The landlord and the sheriff came to drive us all away.
| Bm | D | A7 |
They set my roof on fire with their demon yellow spleen,
| D | | G D |
And that's another reason why I left old Skibbereen.

| D | A7 |
Oh, Father dear, the day will come when vengeance loud will call,
| D | | G D |
And we will rise with Erin's boys and rally one and all.
| Bm | D | A7 |
I'll be the man to lead the van beneath our flag of green,
| D | | G D |
And loud and high we'll raise the cry: "Revenge for Skibbereen!"

The Fenian Man O'War

After the American Civil War there was a great desire among many of the members of the Irish Brigade (Colonel Meagher, its commander, himself an 1848 exile) to strike a blow for Irish freedom. This coincided with the rise of the Fenian movement in Ireland and America. A ship, the *Erin's Hope,* was outfitted in Boston, and it sailed for Ireland in 1867. A few dozen Irish-American officers who landed at Cork in the expectation of commanding an army against England were immediately arrested. That was the only voyage of *Erin's Hope* — the Fenian Man o' War.

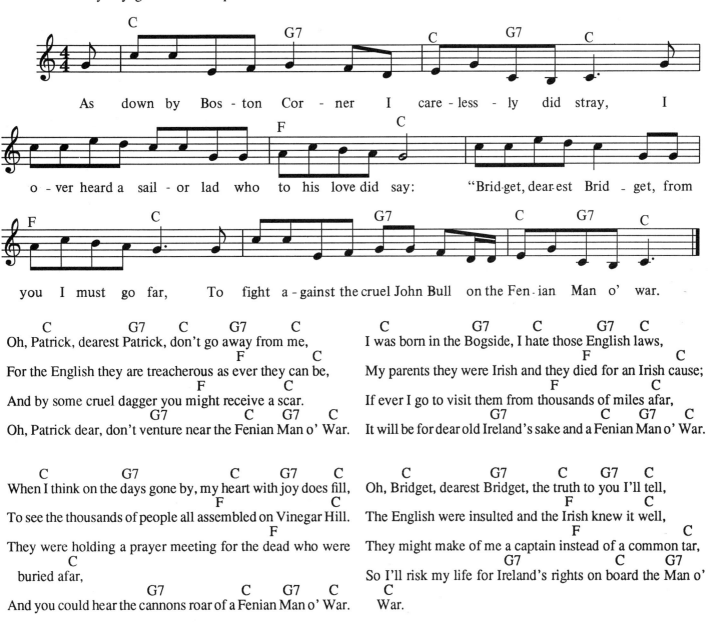

As down by Boston Corner I carelessly did stray, I o-ver heard a sail-or lad who to his love did say: "Brid-get, dear-est Brid-get, from you I must go far, To fight a-gainst the cruel John Bull on the Fen-ian Man o' war.

    C   G7   C   G7   C
Oh, Patrick, dearest Patrick, don't go away from me,
                    F   C
For the English they are treacherous as ever they can be,
             F   C
And by some cruel dagger you might receive a scar.
             G7   C   G7   C
Oh, Patrick dear, don't venture near the Fenian Man o' War.

    C   G7   C   G7   C
I was born in the Bogside, I hate those English laws,
                    F   C
My parents they were Irish and they died for an Irish cause;
             F   C
If ever I go to visit them from thousands of miles afar,
             G7   C   G7   C
It will be for dear old Ireland's sake and a Fenian Man o' War.

    C   G7   C   G7   C
When I think on the days gone by, my heart with joy does fill,
                    F   C
To see the thousands of people all assembled on Vinegar Hill.
                    F
They were holding a prayer meeting for the dead who were
    C
 buried afar,
             G7   C   G7   C
And you could hear the cannons roar of a Fenian Man o' War.

    C   G7   C   G7   C
Oh, Bridget, dearest Bridget, the truth to you I'll tell,
                    F   C
The English were insulted and the Irish knew it well,
                    F   C
They might make of me a captain instead of a common tar,
             G7   C   G7
So I'll risk my life for Ireland's rights on board the Man o'
    C
War.

    C   G7   C G7   C
They both sat down together, then he arose to stand,
                    F   C
A Fenian crew surrounded them, which nearly rowed to land.
                    F   C
Then Patrick raised a Fenian flag and waved it near and far,
             G7   C   G7   C
And Bridget blessed her sailor boy on board the Man o' War.

The Fenians of Cahirciveen

The aim of the Fenian movement was to form a great league of Irishmen in all parts of the world against the rule of Britain in Ireland. To that end they not only conducted activities in Ireland and England, but on two occasions (June 1866 and April 1870) attempted armed invasions of Canada from the United States. Both of these adventures ended disastrously for the Fenians.

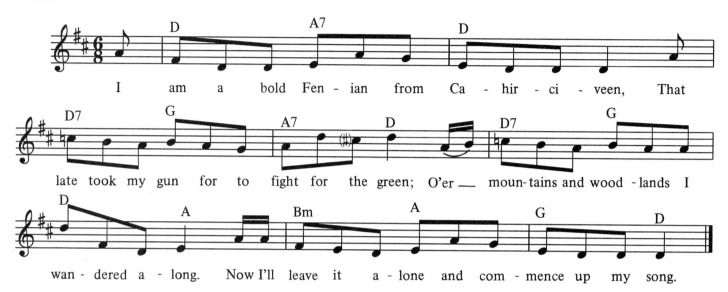

I am a bold Fen - ian from Ca - hir - ci - veen, That late took my gun for to fight for the green; O'er — moun - tains and wood - lands I wan - dered a - long. Now I'll leave it a - lone and com - mence up my song.

```
      D              A7        D
We marched to Kells station that lies near the strand,
    D7      G              A7      D
Where the sea rushes in with great force to the land;
    D7      G           D       A
And then you may say we had courage go leor,
      Bm       A        G        D
When Kells station was taken by the boys of Filemore.

      D         A7       D
We marched all along and our guns we did load,
    D7    G          A7         D
We met a policeman, on horseback he rode.
    D7        G              D       A
We asked him to surrender, but the answer was no,
    Bm        A        G          D
And a ball from young Conway soon levelled him low.

      D           A7       D
Away we marched on and our guns we did load,
    D7      G            A7         D
We met Father Meggan and for him we bowed low.
    D7      G                D        A
He gave us his blessing, saying, "God be your friend
      Bm        A       G        D
In the battle for freedom for which you are bent."
```

```
        D           A7        D
Come shoulder your arms, come march and obey,
      D7        G        A7       D
But alas! we were beaten all on the next day,
      D7       G            D        A
Our plans were found out by some ugly old spy,
        Bm       A        G       D
And on Captain Moriarty they did cast an eye.

        D         A7        D
Moriarty came in on the mail car next day,
      D7       G        A7       D
To lead our brave boys and to join in the fray.
      D7        G            D         A
To our greatest surprise he was marched off to jail,
        Bm       A        G        D
Which left us in sorrow our loss to bewail.

        D          A7          D
Then it's off thro' the mountains we all took our course,
        D7       G        A7       D
Our stomachs being slack and we had not a horse.
      D7    G       D         A
We were in a number about sixty strong
        Bm         A        G          D
Surrounded by redcoats, for something went wrong.
```

```
              D       A7        D
Then hurrah for the Fenians of Cahirciveen,
          D7       G     A7       D
No bolder nor braver in Erin was seen.
          D7      G          D       A
No soldiers more true to the banner of green
              Bm      A      G     A
Than the true-hearted Fenians of Cahirciveen.
```

go leor – galore

The Bold Fenian Men

Elizabethan thoughts on Ireland, Part 2 (1577) — Richard Stanyhurst's "playne and perfecte" description of Ireland: "A conquest draweth, or at the leastwise ought to draw, to it three things, to wit law, apparel and language. For where the country is subdued, there the inhabitants ought to be ruled by the same law that the conqueror is governed by, to wear the same fashion of attire wherewith the victor is vested, and to speak the same language that the vanquisher parleth. And if any of these three lack, doubtless the conquest limpeth."

By Michael Scanlan

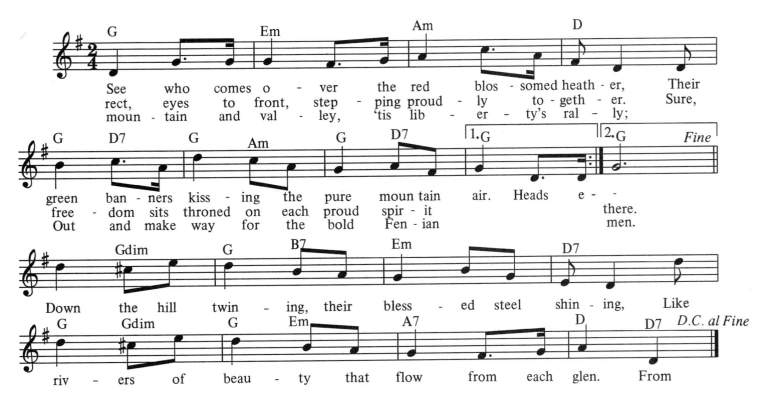

Our prayers and our tears they have scoffed and derided;
They've shut out the sunlight from spirit and mind.
Our foes were united and we were divided,
We met and they scattered our ranks to the wind.
But once more returning, within our veins burning
The fires that illuminated dark Aherlow Glen;
We raise the old cry anew, slogan of Conn and Hugh;
Out and make way for the bold Fenian Men!

We're men from the Nore, from the Suir and the Shannon,
Let tyrants come forth, we'll bring force against force.
Our pen is the sword and our voice is the cannon,
Rifle for rifle and horse against horse.
We've made the false Saxon yield many a red battlefield:
God on our side, we will triumph again;
Pay them back woe for woe, give them back blow for blow-
Out and make way for the bold Fenian Men!

Side by side for the cause have our forefathers battled,
Our hills never echoed the tread of a slave.
In many a field where the leaden hail rattled,
Through the red gap of glory they marched to the grave.
And those who inherit their name and their spirit,
Will march 'neath the banners of Liberty then;
All who love foreign law   Native or Sassanach
Must out and make way for the bold Fenian Men!

Sassanach - pejorative term for the English

103

Batchelor's Walk

On July 26, 1914, nine hundred antiquated German rifles that had been purchased in Hamburg were smuggled into Howth Harbor, near Dublin. The Irish Volunteers took possession of the rifles and were content to disappear with them. But the King's Own Scottish Borderers had been called out, and when an angry crowd appeared on the docks at Batchelor's Walk, the soldiers opened fire, killing four people and wounding thirty-eight.

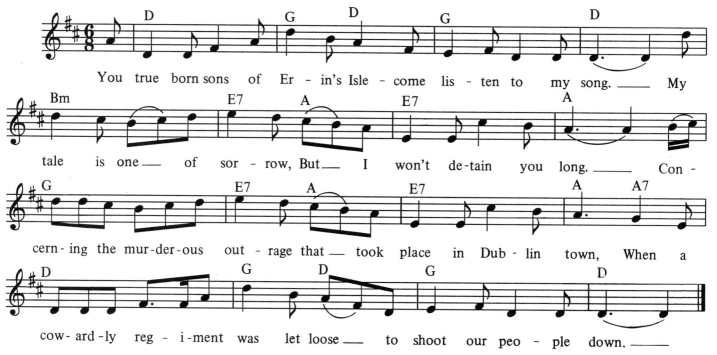

You true born sons of Er - in's Isle - come lis - ten to my song. ___ My tale is one ___ of sor - row, But ___ I won't de-tain you long. ___ Con - cern - ing the mur-der-ous out - rage that ___ took place in Dub - lin town, When a cow - ard -ly reg - i -ment was let loose ___ to shoot our peo - ple down. ___

D　　　　　G　D　　G　　　　D
On the twenty sixth day of July, the truth I'll tell to you,
Bm　　　E7　　　A　　　E7　　　　A
The Irish Volunteers all swore their enemies to subdue,
G　　　　　　E7　　A　　E7　　　　A
They marched straight out to Howth and soon the people were alarmed
A7　D　　　　　G　　　D　G　　　D
When they heard the glorious news, "Our Irish Volunteers are armed."

D　　　　　G　　D　　G　　　D
The crowds they all kept cheering on as our brave defenders passed,
Bm　　　　　E7　　A　E7　　　　A
But their cheers were stopped by an outrage which for some time did last.
G　　　　　E7　　A　　E7　　　　A
Our gallant men, the Volunteers, were met in front and rear,
A7　D　　　　G　　　D　G　　　D
By the King's Own Scottish cowards who are doomed for everywhere.

D　　　　G　　D　　G　　　D
God save our gallant Captain Judge, the hero of the band,
Bm　　　　E7　A　E7　　　　A
Who nearly gave his precious life for the just cause of our land,
G　　　　E7　A　E7　　　　A
In spite of terrible injuries and weak from loss of blood,
A7　D　　　　G　D　　G　　　D
He fondly hugged his rifle grand, the prize of his brotherhood.

D　　　　　G　D　　G　　　　　D
Next in the list of heroes is the scout so well renowned,
Bm　　　　E7　A　E7　　　　　A
With the butt end of his rifle felled a Borderer to the ground,
G　　　　E7　　A　E7　　　　A
He disarmed him of his weapons and soon made his escape,
A7　D　　　　G　　　D　G　　　D
By climbing a wall in Fairview, for his young life was at stake.

D　　　　　　G　D　　G　　　　D
The Dublin Police were ordered the Volunteers for to subdue,
Bm　　　　E7　　A　　E7　　　　A
But O' Neill and Gleeson boldly replied: "Such a thing we decline to do,
G　　　　E7　A　　E7　　　　A
For to fight against our countrymen would on us put a stain,
A7　D　　　　　G　　D　G　　　D
For we wish to see our native land a Nation Once Again."

D　　　　　　G　　　D　　G　　　　D
On Batchelor's Walk a scene took place, which I'm sure had just been planned,
Bm　　　　E7　　A　　E7　　　　A
For the cowardly Scottish Borderers turned and fired without command.
G　　　　E7　A　　E7　　　A
With bayonets fixed they charged the crowd and left them in their gore,
A7　　D　　　G　　　D　G　　　D
But their deeds will be remembered in Irish hearts for evermore.

D　　　　　G　　　D　G　　　　D
God rest the souls of those who sleep apart from earthly sin,
Bm　　　E7 A　　E7　　　　A
Including Mrs. Duffy, James Brennan and Patrick Quinn;
G　　　　E7　A　　E7　　　　A
But we will yet avenge them and the time will surely come,
A7　　D　　　G　　D　　G　　　D
That we'll make the Scottish Borderers pay for the cowardly deeds they done.

The Easter Rebellion

On Easter Monday, April 24, 1916, the Dublin General Post Office was occupied by a Sinn Fein detachment as a part of a hoped-for general Irish uprising. One of its leaders, Padraic Pearse, read out the following declaration from the steps of the Post Office: ". . . We declare the right of the people of Ireland to the owership of Ireland, and to the unfettered control of Irish destinies. . . ." By May 1, the Rising was over—crushed by the British army. By May 12, fourteen of its leaders, including Pearse, had been court-martialed and shot. Suvla Bay and Sud el Bar (actually Sedd el Bahr) are in Gallipoli, Turkey, where in 1915, British and Commonwealth soldiers, including Irish "Wild Geese" troops, landed as part of an unsuccessful attempt to force open the Dardanelles channel and occupy Constantinople. This disastrous undertaking cost Winston Churchill his job as First Lord of the Admiralty.

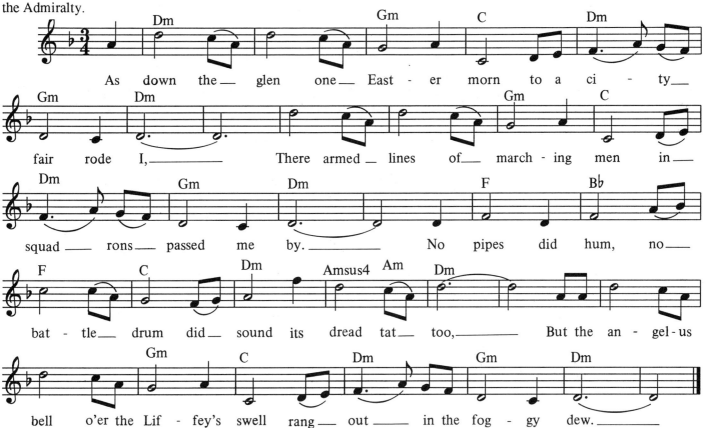

As down the — glen one — East - er morn to a ci - ty — fair rode I,_____ There armed — lines of — march - ing men in — squad — rons — passed me by. _____ No pipes did hum, no — bat - tle — drum did — sound its dread tat — too,_____ But the an - gel - us bell o'er the Lif - fey's swell rang — out _____ in the fog - gy dew. _____

Dm   Gm   C   Dm   Gm Dm
Right proudly high over Dublin Town they hung out the flag of war,
        Gm C   Dm   Gm Dm
'Twas better to die 'neath an Irish sky than at Suvla or Sud el Bar.
       F   Bb   F   C   Dm   Am4 Am   Dm
And from the plains of Royal Meath strong men came hurrying   through,
                    Gm   C   Dm   Gm Dm
While Britannia's sons, with their great guns, sailed in by the foggy dew.

       Dm   Gm C   Dm Gm   Dm
The bravest fell, and the sullen bell rang bell rang mournfully and clear,
              Gm C   Dm   Gm Dm
For those who died that Eastertide in the springing of the year;
       F   Bb   F   C   Dm   Amsus4 Am Dm
And the world did gaze with deep amaze on those fearless men — but few,
                Gm   C   Dm   Gm Dm
Who bore the fight that Freedom's light might shine through the foggy dew.

       Dm   Gm   C   Dm Gm   Dm
'Twas England bade our "Wild Geese" go that small nations might be free,
                 Gm   C   Dm   Gm   Dm
But their lonely graves are by Suvla's waves and the fringe of the grey North Sea;
       F   Bb   F   C   Am4 Am Dm
Oh, had they died by Pearse's side or fought with De Vale - ra too,
               Gm   C   Dm   Gm Dm
Their place we'd keep, where the Fenians sleep, 'neath the hills of the foggy dew.

       Dm   Gm C   Dm   Gm   Dm
Back to the glen I rode again, and my heart with grief was sore,
              Gm   C   Dm   Gm Dm
For I parted then with valiant men I never would see no more.
       F   Bb   F   C   Dm   Am4 Am Dm
But to and fro in my dreams I go, and I kneel and Pray   for you,
                Gm   C   Dm   Gm Dm
For slavery fled, oh, Rebel dead, when you fell in the foggy dew.

The Cork Men and New York Men

Situated in Cork harbor are the islands of Spike and Haulbowline. Fort Westmoreland, on Spike Island, contained large stores of arms and ammunition — a tempting target for the gallant Cork men.

By T. D. Sullivan

The gal-lant Cork men, mixed with New York men, I'm sure their e - quals can-not be

found; For per - se - ver - ing, in deeds of dar - ing, they set men star - ing the world a

round. No spies can match—them, No sen-tries watch them, No spe-cials catch them or mar their

play. While cle-ver Cork men and cute New York men work new sur- pris - es by night and day.

G   D7   G
Sedate and steady, calm, quick and ready,
  D7   G
They boldly enter, but make no din,
   D7   G
Where'er such trifles, as Snider rifles,
    D7   G
And bright six-shooters are stored within.

The Queen's round towers, can't baulk their powers,
    C   G
Off go the weapons by sea and shore,
      D7   G
To where the Cork men and smart New York men
    D7   G
Are daily piling their precious store.

G   D7   G
John Bull, in wonder, with voice like thunder,
    D7   G
Declares such plunder he must dislike;
    D7   G
They next may roll in, and sack Haulbowline,
   D7   G
Or, on a sudden, run off with Spike.

His peace has vanished, his joys are banished,
    C   G
And gay or happy no more he'll be,
     D7   G
Until those Cork men and wild New York men
    D7   G
Are sunk together beneath the sea.

G   D7   G
Oh, bold New York men And daring Cork men,
    D7   G
We own your pleasures should all grow dim,
  D7   G
On thus discerning, and plainly learning
    D7   G
That your amusement gives pain to him.

Yet from this nation, this salutation,
    C   G
Leaps forth, and echoes with thunderous sound
    D7   G
'Here's to all Cork men, likewise New York men,
    D7   G
Who stand for Ireland the world around!'

The Bold Black and Tan

The "Black-and-Tans" (so called for their khaki jackets and black trousers) were largely made up of British soldiers who had been demobilized after World War I. They were sent to Ireland by Prime Minister Lloyd-George, ostensibly to "keep order," but (as Patrick Galvin puts it in his *Irish Songs of Resistance*): ". . . in reality they were what the next generation came to know as fascist stormtroopers." Ian MacPherson was Chief Secretary to the Prime Minister. Major General Sir Nevil MacReady had been London's Commissioner of Police until he was appointed commander-in-chief of the Black-and-Tans, only to be replaced by Sir Hamar Greenwood in April 1920.

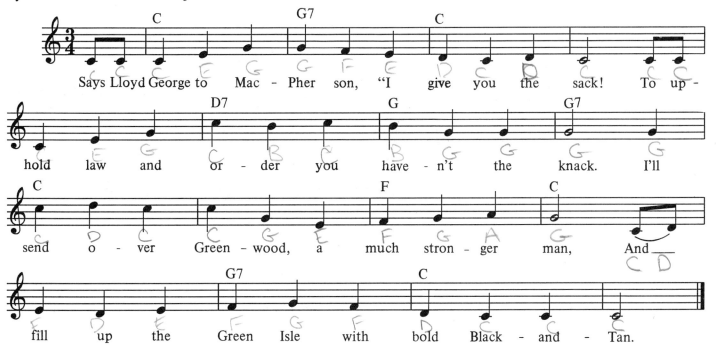

Says Lloyd George to Mac - Pher son, "I give you the sack! To up - hold law and or - der you have - n't the knack. I'll send o - ver Green - wood, a much stron - ger man, And fill up the Green Isle with bold Black - and - Tan.

C	G7	C

He sent them all over to pillage and loot

D7	G	G7

And burn down the houses, the inmates to shoot.

C	F	C

"To re-conquer Ireland," says he, "is my plan,

G7	C

With Macready and Co. and his bold Black-and-Tan."

C	G7	C

From Dublin to Cork and from Thurles to Mayo

D7	G	G7

Lies a trail of destruction wherever they go,

C	F	C

With England to help and fierce passions to fan,

G7	C

She must feel bloody proud of her bold Black-and-Tan.

C   G7   C
The town of Balbriggan they've burned to the ground,
    D7   G   G7
While bullets like hailstones were whizzing around;
   C   F
And women left homeless by this evil clan.
     G7   C
They've waged war on the children, the bold Black-and-Tan.

C   G7   C
Ah, then not by the terrors of England's foul horde,
    D7   G   G7
For ne'er could a nation be ruled by the sword;
   C   F   C
For our country we'll have yet in spite of her plan,
     G7   C
Or ten times the number of bold Black-and-Tan.

C   G7   C
We defeated Conscription in spite of their threats,
    D7   G   G7
And we're going to defeat old Lloyd-George and his pets;
   C   F   C
For Ireland and Freedom we're here to a man,
     G7   C
And we'll humble the pride of the bold Black-and-Tan.

Kevin Barry

On November 1, 1920, Kevin Barry, an 18-year-old student, was hanged in Mountjoy Jail, Dublin. He was the first Irish patriot to be hanged in Ireland since the execution of Robert Emmet in 1803.

Ear - ly on a Sun-day morn - ing, High up - on the gal-lows tree, Kev-in
lad of eight-een sum - mers, Yet there's no - one can de - ny, As he

Bar - ry gave his young - life, For the cause of lib - er - ty. On-ly a
went to death that morn - ing Proud ly

held his head up high, Shoot me fought to free Ire - land!

Chorus

A
"Shoot me like an Irish soldier,
Bm
"Do not hang me like a dog;
E7
"For I fought for Ireland's freedom
A
"On that dark September morn

"All around that little bakery,
Bm
"Where we fought them hand to hand.
E7
"Shoot me like an Irish soldier,
A
"For I fought to free Ireland."

A
Just before he faced the hangman,
Bm
In his lonely prison cell,
E7
British soldiers tortured Barry,
A
Just because he would not tell

All the names of his companions
Bm
Other things they wished to know.
E7
"Turn informer and we'll free you."
A
Proudly, Barry answered, "No!" *Chorus*

A
Calmly standing to attention,
Bm
While he bade his last farewell
E7
To his brokenhearted mother,
A
Whose sad grief no one can tell.

For the cause he proudly cherished,
Bm
This sad parting had to be.
E7
Then he mounted to the gallows,
A
That old Ireland might be free. *Chorus*

A
Another martyr for old Ireland,
Bm
Another murder for the Crown,
E7
Whose brutal laws may kill the Irish,
A
But can't keep their spirits down.

Lads like Barry are no cowards,
Bm
From the foe they will not fly.
E7
Lads like Barry will free Ireland
A
For her sake they'll live and die. *Chorus*

The Irish Free State

On December 6, 1921, the British government agreed to the establishment of the Irish Free State. Strong objections to the treaty were raised by those who resented the prescribed oath of allegiance to the British Crown and to the provision which allowed Northern Ireland to remain outside of the new state. An earlier British government's thoughts on the subject had been expressed by James II, who ruled from 1685 until he was deposed in 1688:

> None but trusty men ought to be put into the garrisons, which need be but few, as Kingsale, Duncannon, Galloway, London Derry, Athlone and Charlemont, which last place should be enlarged to serve for magazine for all the North. 'Tis not safe to lett any of the Natives of Ireland be governors of these above named places, nor to have any troops in them but English, Scots or Strangers, not to tempte temper, and easily led by their Cheefs and Clergy, and bear with great impatience the English yoak, and one cannot beat it into their heads, that several of the Os. and Macks, who were forfited for Rebelling in King James the firsts time, and before, ought to be kept out of their Estates and will allways be ready to rise in arms against the English, and endeavour to bring in Strangers to support them. . . . No Native to be Lord Lieut. nor no Englishman that has an Estate in that Kingdom or great relations there, to be changed every three yeares, to buy no land there.

I went to see Da-vid*, to Lon-don to Da-vid, I went to see Da-vid, and what did he do? He gave me a Free State, a nice lit-tle Free State, a Free State that's tied up with Red, white and Blue

G   Em   Am   D7
I brought it to Dublin to show to Dail Eireann,
G   C   D7   G
I brought it to Dublin and what did they do?
              Em   Am   D7
They asked me what kind a of a thing was a Free State,
G   C   D7   G
A Free State that's tied up with Red, White and Blue.

G   Em   Am   D7
Three-quarters of, Ireland a nation- I told them,
G   C   D7   G
Tied on to the Empire with Red, White and Blue;
                      Em   Am
And an oath they must swear to King George and Queen
D7
Mary,
G   C   D7   G
An oath they must swear to the son-in-law new.

G   Em   Am   D7
I'm teaching them Irish and painting their boxes
G   C   D7   G
All over with green, sure what more can I do?
                  Em   Am   D7
Yet they tell me, they want just an Irish Republic
G   C   D7   G
Without any trimmings of Red, White and Blue!

*David Lloyd-George, British Prime Minister

The Boys from County Cork

By the end of the Anglo-Irish War of 1918–1921, the inevitability of Partition had begun to sink in. The litany of heroes and battles recounted in this song stands in stark contrast to the almost pathetic, questioning last verse.

You've read in his-t'ry's pa-ges of the he—roes of great fame; The deeds they done, the bat-tles won, and how they made their name. But the boys who gave a his-t'ry to the O-range, White and Green, Are the boys who died in Dub-lin town in nine-teen and six-teen.

Chorus:
C   F   C
Meet the boys from Kerry, meet the boys from Clare,
            D7   G7
Dublin, Wicklow, Donegal, and the boys from Old Kildare;
 C   F   C
Boys from the land beyond the seas, from Boston and New York,
     F   C   G7   C
But the boys that beat the Black-and-Tans were the boys from the County Cork.

C   F   C
Cork gave us Mac Sweeney, a hero he did die,
                D7   G7
Wicklow gave us Michael Dwyer in the days so long gone by.
 C   F   C
Dublin gave us Padraic Pearse, MacBride and Cathal Brugh
     F   C G7   C
And America gave us De Valera to lead old Ireland through. Chorus

    C   F   C
We seem to be divided, I really don't know why,
                D7   G7
We've a glorious list of martyrs who for Ireland's cause did die;
   C   F   C
Now why not get together and join in unity,
    F   C   G7   C
The North, the South, the East and West will set old Ireland free. Chorus

Other Irish Music from Mel Bay

Celtic Airs, Jigs, Hornpipes & Reels book/CD set

———

Deluxe Tinwhistle Songbook book

———

Fiddle Tunes & Irish Music for Guitar book/CD set

———

Fiddle Tunes & Irish Music for Mandolin book/CD set

———

Fun with the Tin Whistle book and cassette (Irish tin whistle method)

———

The Irish Dulcimer book

———

The Irish Flute book